Anchored to Success: Strategies for Effective Leadership

Frank M. Kuras

Quill Hawk Publishing

Anchored to Success: Strategies for Effective Leadership

ISBN: 978-1-965142-28-8 (Paperback)
ISBN: 978-1-965142-29-5 (Hardback)

Library of Congress Control Number: 2024923413

Cover designed by Fins and Feathers Designs

Published by Quill Hawk Publishing

To my beloved wife, Maritchil, whose unwavering support, love, and strength have been the foundation of every step forward. Your resilience and compassion inspire me daily, and I am forever grateful to walk this journey with you by my side.

To my daughters, Alexis and Liachell, who fill my life with pride and purpose. Liachell, for carrying on the family legacy with honor as a Naval Officer, and Alexis, for the joy and warmth you bring to our family. You both remind me every day why we serve and strive for a better future.

To my father, Frank, whose love, wisdom, and dedication provided the strong foundation of my upbringing. Your guidance and support taught me the values of integrity, resilience, and respect. Thank you for creating a home filled with love, strength, and encouragement.

To the United States Navy and the Chiefs Mess, thank you for the invaluable leadership, guidance, and camaraderie that have shaped me throughout my career. And to all the Sailors that I have served with, you have taught me what it truly means to lead with integrity and purpose.

And in loving memory of Joseph "Joey" Kuras, whose spirit continues to inspire and strengthen us. May his memory remind us always of the power of love and family.

Table of Contents

Preface

Leadership is communicating, mentoring, influencing, and inspiring individuals or teams to achieve common goals or visions. In short basic terms it's talent management, it's not just positional authority to lead but the ability to influence people emotionally, intellectually, and behaviorally. Leaders do not just manage; they embody values that can transform the potential within a team or organization into successful outcomes. At its core, leadership involves many different aspects, such as vision, decision-making, and emotional intelligence (EI). Vision provides direction, decision-making drives actions, and emotional intelligence ensures the team is motivated and cohesive. Leadership can take many forms: a business executive directing an organization's future, a coach motivating athletes, or a political figure shaping public policy. Regardless of its application, leadership involves inspiring others to contribute towards a goal while maintaining a positive and effective working environment.

Leadership is different in each element, but effective leadership is vital to any organization's success. It directly impacts organizational performance, employee satisfaction, and the overall atmosphere within a team. Leaders set the tone for their teams; effective leaders create a culture promoting trust, collaboration, and accountability. At the same time, toxic leadership establishes the opposite. Influential leaders provide a well-defined vision that aligns with the team's efforts. When leaders articulate a vision, individuals can rally behind a common objective, channeling their energies toward shared goals. Engagement with employees is often the result of skilled leadership. Leaders who actively engage with their teams, understand their needs, and encourage an environment where everyone feels valued and motivated. Influential leaders are often flexible and adaptable. Good leadership in a rapidly changing world involves pivoting strategies, solving problems creatively, and guiding teams through uncertainty. Effective Leaders are also well-versed in holding people accountable while being accountable themselves; this helps create high-performing teams. When leaders model accountability, they create a culture where tasks are completed on time, and individuals take responsibility for their roles.

Innovation thrives under leaders who encourage creative thinking, provide opportunities for risk-taking, and create a safe space for experimentation. Leaders who empower their teams to try new things foster an environment of growth and learning. This significantly influences an organization's culture. A leader who fosters an inclusive, collaborative, and ethical workplace will ensure that employees feel a strong sense of belonging, leading to higher morale and reduced turnover.

While effective leadership can elevate an organization, toxic leadership can have disastrous consequences. Toxic leadership refers to behaviors and styles that are detrimental to the well-being of team members, eroding trust and destroying morale. A toxic leader might micromanage, take credit for others' work, belittle subordinates, or foster a climate of fear and competition rather than collaboration. Under poor leadership, employees often feel demoralized and unmotivated. They may withdraw effort, leading to decreased productivity and innovation. In contrast to effective leadership, which fosters engagement, toxic leadership stifles enthusiasm. In some cases, high turnover rates are a hallmark of toxic leadership. Employees who feel unappreciated or bullied are likelier to leave the organization for a healthier work environment. This increases recruitment costs and disrupts organizational continuity.

Toxic leaders create environments where employees are afraid to speak up or contribute. This leads to a disengaged workforce that is disrespected and burned out. This can decrease productivity, extend timelines on projects and goals, and damage an organization's internal and external reputation. Negative workplace culture leaks into the public, affecting relationships with clients, customers, and potential future employees. Toxic leadership can weaken an organization's foundation, leading to long-term challenges such as financial losses, damaged relationships, and an eroded corporate culture. In contrast, effective leadership builds resilience, fosters loyalty, and maintains a positive momentum that helps an organization achieve sustainable success.

The Navy has exposed me to so many characteristics of leadership and provided me the opportunity to see how each of those characteristics has lead to both excellent and poor leaders. These traits are universal and not only relegated to the military environment. Seeing them in action in the government and corporate world has put the exclamation point on their applicability to anyone in a leadership role.

Understanding what leadership is, the power that comes with it and the tools you have at your disposal will enhance your leadership skills and create your legacy as an effective leader. This book is not only meant to inform but to be used as a guide for leadership development. Consider taking the time after each chapter to evaluate yourself, the leaders you look up to, and those leaders you've seen fail in these leadership areas. Also, consider where you are, where you want to be, and where you DON'T want to be in your leadership journey.

Chapter 1: With Great Power Comes Great Responsibility

Effective leaders have many tools to create, mold, or guide their teams. Many leaders refer to and use the seven powers of leadership. Like any other profession, understanding the use of tools increases the likelihood of success. Leadership isn't a one-size-fits-all concept; it encompasses various sources of influence. John French and Bertram Raven introduced a framework in 1959 that identified five bases of power, which have since expanded to seven powers of leadership. These powers help explain how leaders influence others and why they succeed or fail in getting their teams to follow. Understanding and using all seven powers of leadership helps leaders become more effective in creating successful outcomes.

Legitimate power is power that comes from a position of authority. Leaders with legitimate power, such as CEOs, managers, or team leads, are recognized by their roles and structure. Their authority is formal and comes from the organization itself. However, solely relying on legitimate power without earning respect can lead to minimal effectiveness in leadership.

Expert power is leaders who are highly knowledgeable in a specific field. Their expertise earns them the trust and confidence of their followers. People follow these leaders because they are seen as competent rather than because of their titles. For instance, a skilled engineer leading a team because of their technical mastery would possess expert power.

Referent power stems from personal charisma and the ability to connect with others. Leaders with referent power influence others because people admire, like, or identify with them. This power is personal and emotional rather than based on a position. Charismatic leaders like Martin Luther King Jr. or Nelson Mandela had significant referent power cue to their ability to inspire and uplift others.

Coercive power is derived from the ability to impose punishment or negative consequences. Leaders with coercive power can enforce rules, impose sanctions, or fire employees. However, this form of power is often associated with toxic leadership. While it may work in the short term, coercive power can erode trust, generate resentment, and foster a toxic environment.

Reward power helps leaders offer incentives such as promotions, raises, bonuses, or public recognition. People are motivated by the idea of receiving these rewards, which can reinforce good performance. Effective leaders use reward power strategically to recognize achievements and encourage productivity.

Informational power comes when leaders possess valuable information, insights, or knowledge. This is not the same as expert power, which is based on skills; rather, informational power comes from having access to critical data that others need. A leader may possess vital market research or insider knowledge that puts them in a position of influence.

Connection power relates to networking and relationships with influential people. Leaders who can leverage their contacts and professional relationships to benefit the organization are said to have connection power. For example, a business leader with a strong network of investors can open doors to new opportunities for their organization.

In summary, leadership is more than just a role; it's a dynamic process of influencing, guiding, and nurturing teams. Effective leadership plays a critical role in the success of an organization by fostering engagement, accountability, and innovation. Conversely, toxic leadership can erode the culture and productivity of an organization, leading to high turnover and low morale. By understanding the seven powers of leadership, leaders can assess how they influence their teams and use their power wisely. Effective leadership balances these powers to inspire positive change and growth, ensuring that organizations meet their objectives and maintain a healthy and thriving work environment.

Chapter 2: Effective Communication

Effective communication in leadership is the cornerstone of successful organizations. Leaders who master the art of communication enhance team collaboration and efficiency and inspire and motivate others to achieve common goals. At its core, leadership is about influencing others to achieve a common objective. To do this effectively, leaders must be able to convey their vision, expectations, and goals clearly. Communication is vital in every aspect of leadership, from decision-making and problem-solving to conflict resolution and team building.

Leaders who communicate effectively provide clear direction and set expectations that guide their teams toward achieving objectives. Team members may become confused about their roles without clear communication, leading to inefficiencies and mistakes. Effective communication ensures that everyone understands the organization's mission and their role in accomplishing it. Trust is another fundamental component of leadership; communication is the key to building and maintaining that trust. Leaders who are open, honest, and transparent in their communication foster trust and respect among their team members. Trust enhances cooperation and encourages employees to voice their opinions, leading to better collaboration and innovation.

Great leaders use communication to inspire and motivate their teams. By articulating a compelling vision and sharing emotional stories, leaders can inspire their employees to go outside their comfort zones and strive for excellence. Inspirational communication empowers individuals to believe in their abilities and the value of their contributions.

Communication also plays a critical role in managing and resolving conflicts. Leaders who possess strong communication skills can mediate disputes and help resolve issues before they escalate. Leaders can foster understanding and collaboration by actively listening to all parties involved and encouraging open dialogue, preventing misunderstandings from undermining team cohesion.

While effective communication is crucial for leadership, several barriers can hinder it. Identifying and addressing these barriers is essential for leaders who want to communicate more effectively. In today's globalized workforce, cultural differences can pose significant challenges to communication. Different cultures have different norms, values, and communication styles, which can lead to misunderstandings. For instance, in some cultures, direct communication is valued, while indirect communication is preferred in others. Leaders need to be culturally sensitive and adaptable to navigate these differences effectively.

Emotions such as fear, anger, and frustration can distort communication. Leaders may sometimes withhold information out of fear of conflict or criticism, or team members may feel intimidated and refrain from expressing their opinions. Emotional intelligence, which involves recognizing and managing one's emotions and those of others, is a critical skill for leaders to mitigate emotional barriers.

In organizations with geographically dispersed teams, physical distance and reliance on technology for communication can create barriers. Virtual communication tools such as emails, video conferencing, and instant messaging can lead to misunderstandings due to the absence of non-verbal cues like body language and tone of voice. Leaders must be aware of these limitations and use various communication methods to understand their messages.

Perception is subjective, and individuals may interpret the same message differently based on their experiences, biases, and assumptions. A leader's message might be misunderstood if the audience perceives it through a different lens than intended. Active listening and feedback mechanisms are essential for leaders to ensure their messages are interpreted accurately.

Different leadership styles impact communication in unique ways. Understanding these styles can help leaders adapt their communication approach based on the needs of their teams and organizational goals.

Transformational leaders are known for their ability to inspire and motivate their teams by communicating a compelling vision for the future. They use communication to create a sense of purpose and alignment within the organization. These leaders tend to be charismatic and focus on empowering employees by fostering open communication and encouraging creative input. The transformational style of leadership is particularly effective in driving innovation and change.

Transactional leaders focus on establishing clear expectations and rewarding or punishing employees based on performance. Communication in this leadership style tends to be more formal and directive, emphasizing tasks and outcomes. While this approach can effectively achieve short-term objectives, it may not foster the same level of engagement or creativity as transformational leadership. Transactional leaders should be mindful of balancing task-oriented communication with motivational elements to keep their teams engaged.

Servant leaders prioritize the needs of their team members above their own and focus on developing others. Communication in this leadership style is characterized by active listening, empathy, and support. Servant leaders foster a culture of trust and collaboration where open dialogue and feedback are encouraged. This communication style can enhance team cohesion and loyalty, as employees feel valued and heard.

Autocratic leaders make decisions independently and expect their directives to be followed without question. Communication is often one-way, with little room for input or feedback from team members. While this leadership style may be effective in crises where quick decisions are necessary, it can stifle creativity and reduce employee morale in the long run. Leaders who adopt an autocratic approach should improve communication by soliciting input and fostering a more collaborative environment when appropriate.

Leaders can enhance their communication effectiveness by adopting several key strategies. These strategies involve not only improving how they convey messages but also how they listen and respond to feedback. One of the most important components of effective communication is active listening. Leaders should focus not only on what they are saying but also on understanding the perspectives and concerns of their team members. Active listening involves paying full attention to the speaker, avoiding interruptions, and responding thoughtfully. It also requires asking clarifying questions and summarizing key points to ensure mutual understanding. Much communication occurs through non-verbal cues such as facial expressions, gestures, and posture. Leaders should be aware of the signals they send through their body language and ensure that these cues align with their verbal messages. Non-verbal communication can reinforce a leader's message or create confusion if not used appropriately.

Feedback is a two-way street, and leaders should create opportunities for giving and receiving feedback. Constructive feedback helps team members improve their performance, and receiving feedback allows leaders to understand how their communication is being perceived. Encouraging a culture of feedback promotes transparency and continuous improvement within the organization. Routine feedback enables leaders to identify areas for development, adapt their leadership style, and enhance their skills over time. It is also a tool for conflict resolution; effective communication helps address misunderstandings or conflicts early, minimizing potential disruptions and fostering a positive work environment. Leaders who communicate effectively can better align their team's goals and values with the broader organizational culture, ensuring everyone's focus is in the same direction.

Effective leaders are adaptable and can adjust their communication style based on the audience and situation. Some team members may prefer detailed explanations, while others may thrive with more autonomy. By being flexible and tailoring their communication approach, leaders can better connect with their teams and meet their needs.

Emotionally intelligent leaders are better equipped to handle the complexities of communication. Emotional intelligence involves self-awareness, empathy, and the ability to regulate emotions. Leaders with high emotional intelligence can navigate difficult conversations, manage conflicts, and build stronger team relationships.

360° communication is crucial for effective leadership for several reasons; it allows leaders to receive feedback from multiple sources, such as subordinates, peers, and superiors, creating a comprehensive view of their performance and impact. It improves relationships by engaging in open dialogue, which fosters trust and transparency, strengthening relationships within the team and organization. It also helps make informed decisions by gathering diverse perspectives; this can make better-informed decisions as they have a holistic understanding of the issues and viewpoints. In addition, it encourages a culture of open communication, empowers team members to share ideas and concerns, and promotes ownership and engagement.

Ultimately, leaders who excel at communication will improve team performance and create a positive and productive organizational culture. Effective communication is critical for leaders who want to inspire, motivate, and lead their teams to success. By overcoming barriers to communication and adopting a flexible, empathetic approach, leaders can build trust, resolve conflicts, and foster a collaborative work environment. Understanding how these leadership styles impact your team in communication and implementing strategies such as active listening, feedback, and emotional intelligence can significantly enhance a leader's communication ability. 360° communication supports leaders in building a more collaborative, responsive, and effective organization.

Chapter 3: Be Genuine

Humility and support are vital leadership traits; both are essential because they foster trust, collaboration, and personal growth within a team. Leaders prioritizing humility over ego are more open to learning, approachable, and better suited to create environments where people feel valued and heard. Supportive leaders empower their teams by recognizing individual strengths and providing the resources and guidance needed for collective success. These traits build loyalty, engagement, and a sense of shared purpose, leading to high performance and sustainable success.

Authenticity builds trust, and being a genuine leader means leading with authenticity, transparency, and integrity. Genuine leaders stay true to their values, are honest about their intentions, and cultivate trust by consistently behaving in ways that reflect their core beliefs. This fosters respect and loyalty among team members because people are likelier to follow leaders they perceive as real, trustworthy, and consistent. Conversely, inauthentic leadership, where leaders project a false image or act contrary to their values, can create distrust, disengagement, and a toxic work culture when genuine leaders show their teams that they have nothing to hide. Being open about intentions and making decisions based on clear principles makes it easier for others to trust them. Trust is the foundation of respect and loyalty in any relationship, and consistently authentic leaders will naturally earn it.

Genuine leaders own up to their mistakes and show vulnerability when appropriate. This transparency makes them relatable and more human, strengthening the connection with their team. Authentic leaders foster environments where people feel comfortable expressing their ideas, concerns, and emotions without fear of judgment. This openness encourages more honest feedback and collaboration, strengthening team cohesion. When team members know their leader is straightforward and honest, they are more likely to reciprocate with honesty, fostering a culture of accountability and mutual respect.

Genuine leaders practice what they preach; when a leader's actions align with their words, it sets a powerful example for the team to follow. This integrity earns respect because it demonstrates consistency and dedication to the values the leader promotes. Team members are more likely to mirror a leader's behavior, contributing to a more positive and aligned organizational culture. Respect grows naturally in this environment because people see their leader as a model of the behavior they expect in return.

Authenticity allows leaders to build real connections with their teams. They understand that leadership is not about power or control but about guiding and supporting others. By showing empathy and genuinely caring about the well-being of their team, they foster a deep sense of loyalty. People are more likely to stay committed to leaders who care about them personally and professionally. Authentic leaders inspire loyalty not through fear or authority but through compassion, fairness, and respect.

Genuine leaders articulate a clear set of values and live by them. When team members see their leader is committed to a cause greater than themselves, they are more likely to buy into the vision and work toward common goals. Authentic leadership creates a sense of shared purpose and belonging, strengthening loyalty as team members feel part of something meaningful.

Inauthentic leaders may say one thing and do another or adopt leadership styles they think are expected of them rather than staying true to themselves. This inconsistency erodes trust quickly because people can sense when a leader is disingenuous or acting with hidden agendas. Without trust, teams become disengaged, communication breaks down, and loyalty diminishes. Once lost, trust is extremely hard to rebuild. People are less likely to invest emotionally in leaders who appear to be putting on a facade or leading based on external expectations rather than internal conviction. Employees who sense inauthenticity may become cynical, disengaged, and less motivated to give their best effort. Inauthentic leadership can also lead to a misalignment between the leader and the team, creating an environment where people feel disconnected or unappreciated.

Inauthentic leaders often shift their behavior depending on the situation, trying to please everyone or gain favor. This leads to instability because their teams don't know what to expect. Teams crave consistency, and leaders who constantly change their approaches risk creating confusion and reducing morale. Without a strong sense of self, inauthentic leaders often struggle with decision-making, relying on external validation or trends, leading to poor judgment and reactive leadership. Leaders who lack authenticity may lose credibility with their team because their actions may seem self-serving or misaligned with their stated goals. Without credibility, leaders lose the influence needed to drive change or inspire their teams effectively. This lack of credibility can also hurt the organization's reputation, making attracting or retaining talent difficult and causing further long-term damage.

It is important to align your leadership style with personal values and reflect on your values and beliefs. Ask yourself what principles guide your behavior, what matters most to you, and how you define success professionally and personally. Clarifying what you stand for ensures that your leadership style will be grounded in those values. Use self-assessment tools and reflection or seek feedback from trusted peers or mentors to understand how your values manifest in your leadership style. Different leadership styles, such as transformational, servant, or democratic, align with different values. Be the leader whose style aligns with your core principles and personality rather than trying to emulate a leadership trend or someone else's style. For example, if empathy and collaboration are key values, servant leadership might best fit you. A transformational leadership style might align with your values if innovation and pushing boundaries are important. Authentic leaders ensure that their actions consistently align with their values, even in difficult or high-stakes situations. This consistency is what builds credibility and trust over time. When your behavior reflects your values, people can count on you to act in predictable and moral ways. Leaders prioritizing consistency over popularity or short-term gains are more likely to build a legacy of respect and loyalty.

Be sure to communicate values clearly, and let your team know your values and why they guide your decisions. Leaders who communicate transparently about their motivations and principles foster a culture of openness and understanding. This clarity helps people align their efforts with the organization's broader mission. By modeling your values in everyday interactions, you help others see the connection between your words and actions, reinforcing trust and loyalty.

Part of being an authentic leader is showing vulnerability when appropriate. This doesn't mean oversharing or being overly emotional, but rather being honest when you don't have all the answers or acknowledging mistakes. Vulnerability shows humility and reinforces that you're human, making it easier for others to relate to and trust you.

While being authentic is about staying true to your values, flexibility in your approach is still important. Situations may require different tactics or styles, but the underlying values should remain

19

unchanged. Adapting your leadership style while maintaining core values helps you stay effective without losing authenticity. This balance between adaptability and consistency is key to leading with strength and integrity.

Many leaders have a hard time understanding that confidence and humility can coexist. Balancing the need to showcase success while remaining humble is a critical skill for leaders and professionals alike. On one hand, self-promotion is important for career advancement, visibility, and inspiring others. Conversely, humility helps maintain genuine connections, earn respect, and avoid being arrogant. The key is finding a balance where you highlight your achievements in a way that promotes value while maintaining an attitude of gratitude and openness to learning. Understanding the difference between bragging and showcasing is all about how it's delivered. Sharing successes and accomplishments helps build credibility. It shows you are competent and crucial for gaining influence and leadership roles. When people see tangible evidence of your skills and achievements, they are more likely to trust your judgment and follow your lead. Highlighting your successes can also serve as motivation for others.

When done relatably, sharing how you've overcome challenges or achieved milestones can inspire those around you to pursue their goals with greater confidence and determination. Suppose you don't showcase your abilities and achievements. In that case, you risk being overlooked for opportunities such as promotions, partnerships, or new projects. When done right, self-motivation puts you on the radar of decision-makers looking for someone with your expertise. But remember that overemphasizing your success can create resentment among colleagues and peers, particularly if it comes across as boastful or dismissive of others' contributions. Humility helps maintain harmony and respect within teams, ensuring that successes are celebrated as a shared effort. When discussing your achievements, focus on their impact rather than simply emphasizing your personal role. For example, instead of saying, "I led this project to success," you could say, "This project was a success because we were able to deliver value to the client and solve a key problem for them." This shows your involvement while keeping the focus on the bigger picture, which is more relatable and less self-centered. A simple but effective way to showcase success without sounding arrogant is to use "we" instead of "I" whenever appropriate. This reinforces the idea that accomplishments result from teamwork, even if you played a significant role. By doing so, you maintain a humble tone while still conveying success. When discussing achievements, be specific about the challenges you faced, the actions you took, and the outcomes you achieved. Providing context adds depth to your story and shows that success doesn't come easily. It was the result of hard work, strategic thinking, and problem-solving. Specificity helps people understand the process and value behind success, making it more about the journey and less about self-congratulation. Sometimes, the best way to highlight your success is to let your results talk. Whether through presentations, case studies, or testimonials from clients or peers. Allowing others to recognize your work without constantly reminding them can build a reputation for competence without appearing overly self-promotional. When sharing success, also seek input from others by asking questions like, "What do you think worked well in this project?" or "How can we improve moving forward?". This shifts the conversation from self-promotion to reflection and learning and shows that you're still seeking growth and value the perspectives of others.

Humility fosters deeper, more authentic relationships because it shows you value others' contributions and recognize that success is often a collective effort. People are more likely to trust and engage with leaders who acknowledge their limitations and are open to feedback and collaboration.

Staying humble means acknowledging that you don't have all the answers, which is vital for continuous learning and growth. Arrogance can create blind spots, but humility keeps you open to new ideas and improvement. Recognizing the contributions of others, whether it's your team, a mentor, or other collaborators, helps ground your success in humility. It shows that you appreciate the collective effort and don't view success as a solo achievement. Acknowledging the role of others can also highlight your leadership ability to elevate those around you. Expressing gratitude for the opportunities, support, and people who helped you along the way can humanize your achievements. This shows humility and helps you connect with others on a more personal level. It reminds people that while you may have succeeded, you didn't do it alone.

As Apple's CEO, Tim Cook rarely talks about himself, even though he has been instrumental in the company's success since Steve Jobs' passing. Cook often praises Apple's teams and culture, crediting the collective efforts while maintaining a quiet but authoritative presence in the tech world.

Sheryl Sandberg has also been successful in self-promotion, particularly with her book Lean In. Still, she does so in a way that focuses on helping others. Her approach to self-promotion is largely about elevating the conversation on gender equality and leadership, framing her success as a vehicle for helping others rather than just about personal achievement.

Navigating the balance between showcasing success and staying humble requires consciously focusing on value, collaboration, and the bigger picture. Leaders and professionals who can confidently promote their achievements while remaining grounded and grateful are more likely to earn respect, foster loyalty, and inspire others. By giving credit where it's due, emphasizing the impact of their work, and showing humility in success, individuals can rise to the top without alienating those around them.

Leaders who practice humility and support unlock the potential of their teams. Instead of stifling talent by asserting dominance, they create environments where collaboration, innovation, and trust can flourish. By focusing on the well-being and development of others, these leaders inspire loyalty, foster creativity, and drive long-term success, all while building strong, resilient organizations. A genuine leader fosters respect and loyalty by building trust, promoting open communication, and creating meaningful connections with the team. Authenticity allows leaders to lead by example, inspire commitment to shared values, and maintain credibility even in challenging times. In contrast, inauthentic leadership erodes trust, disengages employees, and undermines a leader's credibility and influence. By aligning their leadership style with their values and maintaining consistency in their actions, leaders can foster long-term loyalty, high morale, and a culture of mutual respect within their organizations.

Chapter 4: Self Awareness

Self-awareness is the foundation of effective leadership; introspection, leadership assessments, and personal growth are key elements in effective leadership. These are cornerstones of effective leadership. Great leaders are focused on understanding and developing their teams and dedicate significant time and effort to improving themselves. Leadership is a continuous journey requiring regular self-reflection, honest assessments, and deliberate personal growth. By focusing on self-awareness, leaders can enhance their effectiveness, make better decisions, and positively impact their organizations.

Introspection refers to looking inward and examining one's thoughts, emotions, and behaviors. For leaders, introspection is essential because it clarifies personal values, strengths, weaknesses, and leadership styles. Self-awareness is the foundation of personal growth, allowing leaders to better understand how their actions influence others and how they can improve. Leaders who regularly engage in introspection develop a clear understanding of their emotions, motives, and behaviors. This awareness helps them make more informed decisions and manage their emotions effectively. Introspection is a critical component of emotional intelligence. By examining their emotional responses to challenges, leaders can improve their ability to manage stress, remain calm, and communicate more effectively. By reflecting on past decisions and outcomes, leaders can identify patterns in their thinking and decision-making processes. This helps them avoid repeating mistakes and improves their ability to make sound judgments. Introspection helps leaders identify areas for growth and improvement, which is essential for continuous development. Recognizing and accepting personal limitations is the first step toward overcoming them. Leaders who regularly schedule time to reflect on their leadership, usually at the end of each day or week, use this time to evaluate decisions, behaviors, and interactions with the team. During this time, writing down your thoughts and experiences is an effective way to engage in introspection. Journaling helps organize thoughts, track progress, and identify areas a leader can improve. Introspection requires honesty, asking yourself difficult questions like, "How come I reacted that way?" or "What should I have done differently?" These questions will help you gain deeper insights into your actions and behavior.

While introspection is a personal process, combining it with external feedback is valuable. Ask trusted colleagues or mentors for honest input on your leadership style and performance. Comparing their perspectives with your reflections can provide a more complete picture.

In addition to introspection, formal leadership assessments are invaluable tools for personal growth. These assessments provide objective data on a leader's strengths, weaknesses, and areas for improvement. Leaders can take targeted actions to improve their skills and effectiveness by identifying key traits and leadership competencies. This assessment gathers feedback from multiple sources, including peers, subordinates, and supervisors. The goal is to provide leaders with a well-rounded view of how others perceive their leadership, highlighting strengths and growth areas. Tools like the Myers Briggs Type Indicator (MBTI) or Strength Based Inventory (SBI) Assessment help leaders understand their personality traits and how these traits influence their leadership style. These assessments can be particularly useful for understanding how to adapt communication and management strategies to different personality types on their team. Emotional intelligence is critical for leadership success. Assessments like the Emotional Quotient Inventory measure leaders' ability to perceive, understand, and manage emotions in themselves and others. Using tools like Clifton Strengths focus on identifying a leader's top strengths and how to leverage them. At the same time, they offer insights into potential blind spots or weaknesses that may hinder leadership effectiveness.

Using all these assessments for growth can help identify patterns, along with strengths and weaknesses, in a leader's style. Use assessments to identify recurring themes in your strengths and weaknesses. For example, suppose multiple assessments indicate a lack of emotional regulation. In that case, you can focus on developing skills like mindfulness or stress management. Set specific goals based on the results of these assessments, which provide a roadmap for improvement. Set specific and measurable goals to enhance your leadership skills based on your results. For example, if an assessment reveals a need for better communication, commit to improving active listening and giving clearer instructions. This happens by creating a development plan. Work with a mentor or coach to create a personal leadership development plan. This plan should include actionable steps to improve identified weaknesses and ways to build on your strengths.

Leadership growth is an ongoing process; revisit assessments regularly to track your progress and adjust your development plan as needed. Doing so ensures continuous improvement and growth. Personal growth in leadership goes beyond simply improving skills. It involves a commitment to lifelong learning, self-improvement, and personal transformation. Effective leaders are those who are continually evolving, both personally and professionally. The best leaders are always learning, whether through formal education, reading, or experiences. They stay open to new ideas and are committed to expanding their knowledge and skill set.

All leaders experience failure, and embracing failure helps leaders grow. Personal growth requires stepping out of your comfort zone, which often involves failure. Rather than fearing failure, great leaders view it as an opportunity to learn and grow. They reflect on mistakes, take responsibility, and use the experience to improve and adapt. As the world changes, so must leaders. Personal growth involves adaptability and willingness to change leadership styles, strategies, and mindsets as circumstances evolve. The ability to adjust is key to staying relevant and effective.

Growth doesn't happen overnight; leaders must practice self-compassion while working through challenges. Being kind to yourself during moments of failure or difficulty helps maintain resilience and long-term progress. Dedicate time to continuous learning for both personal and professional growth. Read books on leadership, attend workshops, and seek new experiences that challenge your thinking and broaden your perspective. Set growth-oriented goals and focus on goals that promote personal growth rather than just professional achievements. For example, work on becoming a better communicator or developing more patience with your team. Practice self-help techniques; mindfulness helps leaders stay present and aware of their emotions, thoughts, and behaviors. Regular mindfulness practice can increase self-awareness and improve emotional regulation, both essential for personal growth. Personal growth requires breaking free from old habits and limiting beliefs. Regularly challenge your assumptions about yourself and others to foster a mindset of openness and curiosity.

Before you can effectively lead others, you must first learn to lead yourself. Self-leadership involves taking responsibility for your development, actions, and mindset. It's about setting a personal example of discipline, integrity, and accountability that others can follow. Self-leadership requires setting high standards for yourself and holding yourself accountable to those standards. This discipline is reflected in your work ethic, time management, and ability to stay focused on your goals. Leaders must be able to self-motivate; effective leaders don't wait for external motivation to act. Internal goals and values drive them, and they can motivate themselves to push through challenges. Self-leaders take ownership of their actions, decisions, and mistakes. They don't blame others or external circumstances for their shortcomings; instead, they take responsibility and work to improve. Just as leaders create a vision for their team, self-leaders have a clear vision for personal and professional growth. They set goals and develop a roadmap for achieving those goals.

Define your values and set personal standards for behavior and performance. These standards should reflect the type of leader you aspire to be and guide your decisions and actions. Make these standards routine; successful self-leadership often starts with daily routines reinforcing positive habits. Establish routines that promote discipline, such as morning reflection, regular exercise, or scheduled time for personal development. Great leaders hold themselves accountable; self-leadership means holding yourself accountable to your goals and commitments. If you fall short, reflect on what went wrong and how to improve next time.

Self-leaders also commit to being lifelong learners and actively seek ways to improve themselves. This may involve learning new skills, improving emotional intelligence, or working on areas of weakness. They recognize and celebrate personal achievements and progress. Celebrating small victories reinforces positive behavior and motivates continued growth.

Introspection, leadership assessments, and personal growth are fundamental to effective leadership. Leaders can enhance their self-awareness and emotional intelligence by reflecting on their actions, seeking feedback, and committing to continuous improvement. This, in turn, makes them more effective at leading others. Self-leadership, which is rooted in personal responsibility and discipline, ensures that leaders set the right example for their teams through a focus on personal growth and self-reflection.

Chapter 5: Self Assessments

Regular reflection is vital for leadership growth; using self-assessments enhances leadership growth and evolution. It allows leaders to reflect on their actions, gain insight into their strengths and weaknesses, and adjust their strategies to improve effectiveness. Regular self-evaluations help leaders stay aligned with their values, develop emotional intelligence, and continuously refine their leadership skills. Several effective self-assessment methods include journaling, 360° feedback, and goal tracking. When used together, these tools provide a comprehensive picture of a leader's performance and areas for improvement.

Journaling is one of the simplest yet most powerful tools for self-assessment. Writing down thoughts, experiences, and reflections allows leaders to process their emotions, review their actions, and gain deeper self-awareness. By regularly journaling, leaders can track patterns in their behavior, recognize their achievements, and identify areas for improvement. Writing down thoughts forces leaders to articulate their feelings, reactions, and decisions, helping them process complex situations more effectively. Journals record past actions, decisions, and emotions, allowing leaders to review their growth over time. Journaling helps leaders reflect on their behaviors, identify what drives them, and recognize emotional triggers. By writing about challenges, leaders can gain new perspectives and generate solutions. Setting aside time at the end of each day or week to reflect on leadership moments, such as interactions with team members, decisions made, and challenges faced, helps create future outcomes. Consider asking yourself questions like "What went well today?" "What could I have done differently?" or "How did I handle a difficult situation?" These prompt deeper self-reflection. Regularly review past entries to identify patterns in your leadership style. This helps you see how you've grown and where you can improve.

360° feedback is a formal method of self-assessment where feedback is gathered from a leader's peers, subordinates, and supervisors. This approach provides a comprehensive view of a leader's performance from different perspectives, highlighting strengths and areas needing improvement. By gathering feedback from multiple sources, leaders can better understand how their behavior impacts others and how they are perceived across different levels of the organization. Often, leaders are unaware that certain aspects of their behavior may affect team dynamics or hinder performance. 360° feedback can uncover these blind spots, offering growth opportunities. This type of feedback creates a sense of accountability, as leaders must address the perceptions and concerns raised by their colleagues. When requesting feedback, ensure that the feedback is encouraged to be open and honest. Ask colleagues to provide constructive feedback on specific areas of your leadership, such as communication, decision-making, or conflict resolution. Once feedback is gathered, look for consistent themes or patterns in the responses. Pay attention to both positive feedback and areas for improvement.

Based on the feedback, identify specific actions you can take to address any shortcomings. For example, suppose feedback suggests you need to improve your listening skills. In that case, you can commit to practicing active listening techniques during meetings. After implementing changes based on feedback, check back with your team or peers to see if they notice improvements. This creates a feedback loop that supports continuous growth. Setting goals and regularly tracking progress is another crucial aspect of self-assessment for leaders. Goal tracking allows leaders to focus on specific areas of improvement and measure their success over time. It provides direction and accountability, helping leaders align with personal and professional development objectives. Setting clear goals gives leaders a sense of purpose and helps them prioritize their efforts. By tracking progress toward specific goals, leaders can objectively assess how well they are improving over time. Goal tracking encourages leaders to take ownership of their development. Knowing that progress will be measured keeps leaders motivated to stay on course. Reaching small milestones provides a sense of accomplishment and encourages further growth. Ensure that your goals are Specific, Measurable, Achievable, Relevant, and

Timebound (SMART). For example, a goal might be to "improve team communication by conducting weekly feedback sessions within the next three months." Break down larger goals into smaller, achievable milestones; this helps maintain motivation and provides regular opportunities to celebrate progress. Use a tool or system to track your progress toward each goal. This could be as simple as a spreadsheet or as structured as goal-tracking software.

Periodically review your goals and assess whether they need to be adjusted based on changes in your circumstances or new feedback. Be flexible and willing to update your goals as you grow. Regular self-assessment enables leaders to evolve in several ways. By continuously reflecting on their actions, gathering feedback, and tracking progress, leaders can finetune their leadership approach and make necessary adjustments to remain effective. Self-assessment ensures that leaders never become complacent. Regular reflection, feedback, and goal setting provide a continuous cycle of improvement, where leaders always strive to become better versions of themselves. Over time, this leads to mastery of leadership skills and a deeper understanding of influencing and inspiring others.

Leadership is as much about managing emotions as it is about making strategic decisions. By regularly evaluating their emotional responses and behaviors, leaders develop emotional intelligence. They become better at recognizing and regulating their emotions, improving their ability to communicate effectively, resolve conflicts, and build strong relationships with their teams. Adaptability is a crucial leadership trait in today's rapidly changing business environment. Self-assessment encourages leaders to remain open to change, learn from feedback, and adapt their approach to different situations. Leaders who regularly evaluate their performance are more likely to embrace new challenges, pivot when necessary, and lead their teams through uncertainty.

One of the most important outcomes of self-assessment is increased self-awareness. Leaders who understand their strengths, weaknesses, and blind spots can play to their strengths while actively working to address their weaknesses. This self-awareness helps leaders build trust with their teams, as they are seen as authentic and transparent in their leadership approach. Self-assessment only works if you're honest with yourself. Be willing to confront uncomfortable truths about your leadership style and areas for improvement. Don't limit feedback to direct reports, seek input from various sources, including peers, mentors, and even customers or clients, to get a well-rounded view of your performance. Self-assessment is a continuous process, not a one-time activity. Stay committed to regularly evaluating your performance and updating your goals. Growth takes time, so it's important to celebrate your wins along the way. Recognizing progress motivates you to keep improving.

Self-assessment is a powerful method for leadership development, enabling leaders to reflect on their performance, gather feedback, and track their progress over time. By using methods such as journaling, 360° feedback, and goal tracking, leaders can identify areas for improvement, measure their success, and evolve into more effective and emotionally intelligent leaders. Leaders who prioritize regular self-assessment improve their skills and inspire their teams to grow and perform at their best.

Chapter 6: Know Your People

Knowing your people is key to leading effectively and using some previously discussed strategies. Empathy, emotional intelligence, and strong relationships are essential for effective leadership. These skills help leaders understand their teams personally, leading to higher levels of trust, motivation, and collaboration. By connecting with their people meaningfully, leaders can create a work environment where individuals feel valued, understood, and supported.

Empathy is the ability to understand and share the feelings of team members. It allows leaders to step into their team members' shoes and view situations from their perspectives. This skill is crucial for building trust and strong relationships, as it demonstrates that a leader genuinely cares about the well-being of their people. Leaders who express empathy build trust within their team. When employees feel their leader understands their struggles, challenges, and emotions, they are more likely to trust them. Trust is the foundation of any strong relationship and is essential for team cohesion. Empathetic leaders create a work environment where individuals feel seen and valued, which boosts morale and engagement. People are likelier to go the extra mile for a compassionate and understanding leader. Empathy allows leaders to approach problems with a deeper understanding of their team's concerns and needs, leading to more thoughtful and effective solutions. Satya Nadella, CEO of Microsoft, is widely recognized for his empathetic leadership style. When he became CEO, Microsoft was perceived as a highly competitive, sometimes toxic workplace. Nadella's empathetic approach focused on creating a culture of collaboration and learning. He encouraged employees to be open about their challenges and emotions, which led to a more compassionate and innovative work environment. His focus on empathy has helped transform Microsoft's culture and contributed to its resurgence as a global tech leader.

Another factor is emotional intelligence (EI), which is to the ability to recognize, understand, manage, and influence one's own emotions and the emotions of others. Leaders with high emotional intelligence can navigate complex interpersonal dynamics, manage stress, and maintain a positive and productive work environment. This is developed by having good self-awareness. Leaders with high EI know their emotions and how they affect their behavior and decision-making. This self-awareness allows them to manage their emotions effectively, preventing reactive or impulsive decisions. EI enables leaders to remain calm under pressure and avoid emotional outbursts, which helps maintain stability and confidence in the team. Emotional intelligence also includes the ability to notice emotional cues from others and understand the social dynamics within a team. This awareness helps leaders manage relationships more effectively and ensure that people feel supported. EI is directly linked to better communication; high EI leaders are skilled in communicating in ways that resonate with different individuals, fostering clarity, reducing misunderstandings, and enhancing teamwork. Oprah Winfrey is often cited as a leader with exceptional emotional intelligence. Her ability to connect deeply with people, understand their emotions, and communicate with authenticity has been a key factor in her success. Whether on her talk show or in her leadership at the Oprah Winfrey Network (OWN), Oprah's emotional intelligence allows her to build strong, trusting relationships with her team and audience. She is known for her communication and listening skills. This combined with the ability to empathize with people from all walks of life, make her a beloved and effective leader.

Knowing your people requires building relationships and fostering a connected and engaged team. Building strong, genuine relationships with team members is a cornerstone of effective leadership. Relationships are built on trust, mutual respect, and open communication. Leaders who take the time to get to know their team members as individuals can create a work environment where people feel valued and supported, which leads to higher morale, loyalty, and productivity. Relationship building is vitally important to foster and encourage teamwork and collaboration because individuals feel more comfortable communicating openly and relying on one another. Building a team and retaining your people are metrics or signs of a leader's effectiveness. People are more likely to stay with an organization if they feel a personal connection to their leader and colleagues. Leaders who build strong relationships can reduce turnover and create a more stable workforce.

Employees who have positive relationships with their leaders are happier in their roles. This satisfaction leads to higher engagement and performance, as individuals feel motivated to contribute to the team's success. Richard Branson, the founder of Virgin Group, is known for his people-first leadership style, which centers on building strong relationships with his employees. Branson famously said, "Take care of your employees, and they'll take care of your business." He invests time in getting to know his employees personally, understanding their passions, and creating a fun, supportive work environment. This approach has built a loyal workforce and contributed to the success of his many ventures. Branson's focus on relationship building has created a culture of mutual respect and camaraderie across the Virgin companies.

Leaders who excel in empathy, emotional intelligence, and relationship building often use these skills to handle difficult situations gracefully and effectively. During the COVID-19 pandemic, Jacinda Ardern, Prime Minister of New Zealand, became globally admired for her empathetic leadership. Ardern communicated clearly and compassionately with the public, frequently expressing understanding of the sacrifices people made.

Her empathetic approach and decisive action, built trust and a sense of unity within New Zealand, helping the country manage the pandemic more effectively than many others.

Having increased EI can help navigate conflict. Sheryl Sandberg, COO of Facebook, has been known to use emotional intelligence to navigate difficult internal conflicts and maintain the company's focus during challenging times. After her husband's sudden death, Sandberg opened up to her team about her grief, modeling vulnerability and emotional intelligence. Her ability to manage her emotions and express them openly helped strengthen her relationships with her team and foster a culture where emotional support was valued. At Pixar, cofounder Ed Catmull has long emphasized the importance of building strong relationships within creative teams to drive innovation. He established a culture where everyone, from directors to animators, could offer feedback and share ideas without fear of judgment. Catmull's relationship-building efforts created a collaborative environment where the best ideas could flourish, resulting in some of the most successful animated films of all time, including Toy Story and Finding Nemo.

Empathy, emotional intelligence, and relationship building are interconnected and mutually reinforcing. Leaders who practice empathy are more likely to develop emotional intelligence because they are attuned to others' emotions and can manage their responses effectively. This emotional intelligence, in turn, helps leaders build stronger relationships by fostering trust, communication, and collaboration. When leaders show genuine empathy, they build trust and rapport with their team, making it easier to establish strong, lasting relationships. Leaders with high emotional intelligence can better identify when empathy is needed and adjust their communication and behavior to meet the emotional needs of their team. As leaders build relationships, they gain a deeper understanding of their team members' personalities, strengths, and challenges, which allows them to further develop their emotional intelligence and empathy.

Leaders prioritizing empathy, emotional intelligence, and relationship-building create an environment where people feel valued, understood, and motivated. These qualities are critical for building trust, driving collaboration, and maintaining a positive and productive workplace. Leaders like Nadella, Winfrey, Branson, and Ardern demonstrate that the ability to connect with people on a personal level is not just a "nice to have" trait. It is a strategic advantage that fosters loyalty, innovation, and long-term success.

Chapter 7: Motivation

Knowing what drives people is vital to effective leadership; motivation is the force that drives individuals to act and achieve goals. Great leaders understand that different people are motivated by different factors, which can be broadly categorized as intrinsic and extrinsic motivators. Intrinsic motivation comes from within, driven by personal satisfaction or fulfillment. In contrast, extrinsic motivation is fueled by external rewards or recognition. Understanding what motivates individuals within your team helps increase the effectiveness of your motivation.

Intrinsic motivation is rooted in personal values, interests, and internal satisfaction. Leaders who tap into this type of motivation help their teams find meaning and purpose in their work, which can lead to higher engagement, creativity, and sustained effort. Giving team members the freedom to make decisions and manage their work fosters a sense of ownership. When people feel in control, they are more likely to be invested in the outcome. Google's example of their "20% time" policy allows employees to spend 20% of their time at work on passion projects that aren't necessarily tied to their core responsibilities. This autonomy encourages creativity and innovation. Projects like Gmail and Google News were born from this strategy, illustrating how intrinsic motivation can drive groundbreaking ideas.

People are often motivated to develop skills and improve their competence. Effective leaders promote this mastery by providing learning opportunities, challenges, and feedback that enable continuous growth. Satya Nadella, the CEO of Microsoft, has shifted the company's culture toward a "growth mindset," where learning and improvement are emphasized. He encourages employees to take risks and learn from failures, which has helped Microsoft regain its innovative edge. Nadella promotes mastery by creating an environment where learning is valued as much as achieving results.

Create purpose: leaders understand that people are more intrinsically motivated when they believe their work has a larger meaning or impact beyond personal gain. Leaders who connect the work to a broader mission can ignite passion and commitment in their teams. Elon Musk, CEO of Tesla and SpaceX, frequently communicates the larger mission behind his companies: to reduce the reliance on fossil fuels and make life multi-planetary. Musk's ability to articulate a compelling vision of the future motivates his teams to work tirelessly, often amid immense challenges, because they believe they are contributing to something world changing.

Extrinsic motivation comes from external factors such as rewards, recognition, or fear of punishment. While intrinsic motivation can lead to deeper engagement, extrinsic motivators are also important in driving short-term results and maintaining performance in certain contexts.

One extrinsic motivation that drives many is financial incentives. Salary increases, bonuses, and other financial rewards can be powerful motivators, especially when linked to performance. These rewards provide a tangible benefit that encourages employees to meet specific goals or expectations. One group under this type of motivation is sales teams that operate under commission-based pay structures, where a portion of their income is tied directly to their performance. The promise of higher earnings for reaching or exceeding sales targets is a classic example of extrinsic motivation driving competitive, goal-oriented behavior.

When financial incentives are not a motivator, many require recognition, praise, or rewards. Public recognition, praise, and awards can boost morale and motivation by satisfying people's desire for acknowledgment. Leaders can foster a positive culture by regularly recognizing efforts, achievements, and contributions. Howard Schultz, the former CEO of Starbucks, built a culture of recognition. He emphasized employee appreciation by offering benefits like stock options to baristas and frequently recognizing team members' hard work. Schultz's leadership was based on the belief that if you take care of your employees, they will take care of your customers. His focus on recognition helped Starbucks build a loyal and motivated workforce.

One motivator indirectly linked to the two above would be career advancement opportunities. Offering promotions, title changes, or opportunities for advancement, even if it doesn't come with financial gains, can motivate people to perform well, as these extrinsic rewards often symbolize success, status, and career progression. Under Jack Welch's leadership, General Electric (GE) was known for its rigorous evaluation system that categorized employees into three groups: top performers, middle performers, and underperformers. Top performers were rewarded with promotions and leadership opportunities, encouraging a high-performance culture and extrinsically motivated people to strive for excellence.

Another strategy used is external pressures, such as deadlines or accountability to others; this can push people to complete tasks and meet objectives. While it may not always foster deep engagement, it ensures timely results and compliance. The film industry operates under strict deadlines, particularly regarding production schedules and release dates. Directors, producers, and teams are motivated to meet these deadlines because of contractual obligations, financial penalties, and the public nature of their work. This extrinsic motivation ensures that projects are completed on time, even under stressful circumstances.

The most effective leaders understand that balancing intrinsic and extrinsic motivators is essential to their team's success. Too much reliance on extrinsic rewards can lead to burnout, decreased job satisfaction, and people doing the bare minimum to earn their reward. On the other hand, only focusing on intrinsic motivators may not be enough to drive short-term performance or push people to achieve stretch goals. Combining autonomy with accountability (intrinsic motivators) fosters creativity and ownership while combining it with external deadlines (an extrinsic motivator) ensures that teams remain productive and goal oriented. This balance encourages both innovation and performance. Atlassian, an Australian software company, uses "ShipIt Days," where employees can work on any project for 24 hours, provided they can deliver a working prototype or solution. This strategy combines autonomy with the extrinsic motivation of presenting tangible results, promoting creativity and accountability. Leaders can recognize individual and team achievements (extrinsic) while emphasizing the impact of the work on the broader mission (intrinsic). This approach not only rewards good performance but reinforces the importance of the work itself. Patagonia, the outdoor clothing company, blends intrinsic and extrinsic motivation. Employees are deeply connected to the company's mission of environmental sustainability, providing intrinsic motivation. Simultaneously, the company offers generous benefits and publicly recognizes team members contributing to impactful initiatives, blending recognition with purpose.

Great leaders, such as Nelson Mandela, inspire teams. Mandela's intrinsic motivation strategy was rooted in purpose. He inspired his followers by emphasizing the greater cause of ending apartheid and building a united South Africa. His leadership was not based on external rewards but on the deep sense of purpose and justice that he instilled in his people. Another is Indra Nooyi, a former CEO of

48

PepsiCo. Nooyi was known for her use of both intrinsic and extrinsic motivators. She often praised her team publicly and provided financial rewards for performance. However, she also communicated a larger vision for PepsiCo, focusing on sustainability and global health, which gave her employees a sense of purpose and mission beyond profit. Richard Branson, founder of Virgin Group, is an expert in using autonomy (intrinsic motivation) and recognition (extrinsic motivation). He famously empowers his employees to take risks and make decisions while celebrating their successes. His leadership creates a culture where employees feel autonomous and appreciated, driving engagement and performance.

Motivation is complex and multifaceted, requiring leaders to skillfully balance intrinsic and extrinsic strategies. By tapping into internal drivers like autonomy, mastery, and purpose alongside external rewards such as recognition, financial incentives, and accountability, great leaders can inspire their teams to achieve extraordinary results.

Chapter 8: Feedback

Constructive feedback is the currency of growth; giving and receiving feedback is one of the most critical aspects of leadership. It is a powerful tool for growth, development, and maintaining open lines of communication within a team. However, feedback must be handled carefully regarding how it is delivered and received. Feedback can inspire positive change, increase performance, and strengthen relationships when done correctly. Conversely, poorly delivered feedback can lead to defensiveness, conflict, and stunted development. Feedback is essential for continuous personal and professional development. For leaders and teams alike, feedback provides insights into performance, behavior, and areas for improvement. It helps people understand how their actions align with expectations and what changes are needed to grow. For example, when employees receive constructive feedback, they can make necessary adjustments, which improves their skills and contributes to overall team performance. Leaders who solicit feedback about their leadership style can improve their decision-making, communication, and effectiveness.

Regular feedback fosters a culture of trust and transparency. When leaders are open to receiving feedback, they value others' perspectives and are committed to improving themselves. Giving feedback regularly, both positive and constructive, demonstrates that a leader is engaged, attentive, and invested in their team's development. In addition, feedback holds people accountable for their actions and performance. Leaders who consistently give feedback ensure that employees know where they stand about their goals. This level of accountability helps teams stay on track, meet expectations, and make necessary adjustments to improve performance. Feedback is crucial for fostering an environment of experimentation and innovation. Employees are more willing to take risks and think creatively when they know they will receive constructive feedback rather than harsh criticism. By creating a safe space for feedback, leaders encourage their teams to innovate and grow.

Giving feedback encouraging development rather than causing defensiveness requires a thoughtful and strategic approach. There are several techniques leaders can use to ensure their feedback is constructive and leads to positive change. The "sandwich" technique delivers feedback by sandwiching constructive criticism between two positive comments. This helps soften the impact of the criticism and ensures the recipient feels valued. A positive example would be, "I appreciate how dedicated you've been to the project and the creative ideas you've contributed." While a constructive one would be, "One area we could improve is meeting deadlines. There have been a few instances where deliverables were delayed, which affected the team's progress. Let's work on time management to stay on track." Leaders should be specific and focused on behaviors, not personalities. When giving feedback, it's essential to focus on specific behaviors rather than making general or personal statements. Feedback should address actions and outcomes, not the individual's character. This helps prevent defensiveness and makes it easier for the person to act on the feedback. Instead of saying, "You're always late," say, "I've noticed that you've been late to three meetings this month, and it s caused delays in our discussions. Can we work on ensuring that you arrive on time so the meetings can be more efficient?" Using "I" statements when delivering feedback helps frame the conversation in a less accusatory way and more about the impact of the behavior on you or the team. This minimizes defensiveness and keeps the feedback objective. Instead of saying, "You never listen to my ideas," say, "I feel like my suggestions aren't being fully considered during our discussions, and I'd like to collaborate more on brainstorming solutions." For feedback to be effective, it should be given promptly. Waiting too long to provide feedback diminishes its impact and relevance. Deliver feedback as close to the event or behavior, if feasible, while ensuring you've had time to gather your thoughts. If a team member performs poorly on a presentation, don't wait until their next review cycle to provide feedback. Instead, address the issue shortly after the presentation, while it's still fresh in their mind, and offer guidance for improvement.

Feedback should be a conversation, not a monologue. Encourage the recipient to share their perspective, ask questions, and engage in the process. This helps clarify any misunderstandings and empowers the individual to take ownership of their growth. After giving feedback, ask, "How do you feel about what I've shared?" or "What are your thoughts on how we can improve in this area together?" When giving constructive feedback, always focus on solutions and growth opportunities rather than solely pointing out what went wrong. Help the person see how they can improve and offer support in making those changes. Instead of saying, "Your report was incomplete and lacked detail," say, "I noticed some key details were missing. Let's enhance your attention to detail by creating a checklist of important items to include in future reports."

Effective leaders learn to balance positive and constructive feedback. Consistently recognizing what someone is doing well helps build morale and makes it easier for people to accept constructive criticism. If feedback is overly negative, it can discourage the recipient and lead to defensiveness. "Your ability to handle client communications has been excellent, and your rapport with them is strong. To take it to the next level, we could work on refining your negotiation approach. Let's discuss strategies to make that more effective."

A leader's ability to receive feedback is just as important as giving feedback. Leaders open to receiving constructive criticism demonstrate humility and a commitment to self-improvement. When receiving feedback, avoid becoming defensive and keeping emotions under control. Listen carefully to what is being said, even if it's uncomfortable. Feedback is a valuable opportunity to learn about how others perceive your actions and identify areas for improvement. If feedback is unclear, ask for clarification; this helps ensure you fully understand the feedback and provides an opportunity to learn more about how your actions affect others. When unclear, ask, "Could you give me an example of when you noticed I wasn't being as communicative as needed? I want to better understand how I can improve." This will give clear examples of how you can improve. Take time to reflect on the feedback before responding. This allows you to process and determine how to apply the information to improve your performance or leadership style. Even if the feedback is difficult to hear, express gratitude to the person providing it; feedback is a gift. Acknowledge their effort in helping you grow and let them know you value their perspective. For example, "Thank you for sharing that with me. I appreciate your honesty, and I'll take some time to reflect on how I can improve in that area."

Finally, demonstrate that you value feedback by acting on it. If someone has given you constructive criticism, make the necessary changes. This helps you grow and shows others that their feedback is being heard and valued. When Satya Nadella became CEO of Microsoft, he focused on transforming the company's culture by fostering a "growth mindset" where feedback was central. He emphasized the importance of giving and receiving feedback to drive continuous improvement. Under his leadership, Microsoft encouraged employees to view feedback as an opportunity for learning rather than criticism. This cultural shift helped Microsoft regain its position as a leading tech company by promoting innovation, collaboration, and personal growth.

Ray Dalio, founder of Bridgewater Associates, implemented a unique approach to feedback called "radical transparency," where employees at all levels are encouraged to give and receive candid feedback. Dalio believes transparency and open feedback are essential for individual and organizational growth. At Bridgewater, feedback is accepted and expected, creating a culture where people constantly learn from each other.

Giving and receiving feedback is an essential practice for effective leadership. Constructive feedback helps individuals and teams grow, fosters a culture of trust and accountability, and drives continuous improvement. Leaders must master the art of delivering feedback in a way that encourages development, focusing on behaviors, being specific, and fostering a two-way dialogue. Additionally, leaders should embrace feedback as an opportunity for self-improvement and growth, demonstrating humility and a willingness to learn. When feedback is given and received effectively becomes a powerful catalyst for both personal and organizational success.

Chapter 9: It's Not Them, Attitude Reflects Leadership

Team dynamics often mirror leadership, which is why a leader's attitude and behavior are pivotal in setting the tone for the entire team. This can influence team morale, work culture, productivity, and long-term success. Leaders are role models, and their demeanor often becomes the benchmark for how team members interact, collaborate, and approach their work. A positive and constructive attitude fosters an environment where employees feel motivated, valued, and empowered. Conversely, a negative or dismissive attitude can lead to low morale, disengagement, and conflict.

A leader's daily actions and behaviors shape the organization's culture. If a leader consistently shows respect, empathy, and accountability, these traits will be mirrored across the team. Team members take cues from leaders on how to behave, how to treat each other, and what is valued in the workplace. For example, a leader who prioritizes collaboration and open communication encourages a culture of trust and transparency.

A leader's attitude directly affects the mood and energy of the team. A positive, optimistic leader can inspire enthusiasm and resilience, even in challenging times. On the other hand, a leader who is constantly stressed, critical, or negative can create a tense and demoralizing environment. Leaders who are calm under pressure and maintain a can-do attitude help the team stay focused and motivated to overcome obstacles. They set the standard for work ethic through their behavior. The team will likely follow suit if a leader demonstrates commitment, punctuality, and a strong sense of responsibility. Conversely, suppose a leader is frequently late, disengaged, or unwilling to put in extra effort. In that case, team members may adopt similar behaviors, leading to a decline in overall performance. Leaders who model accountability by owning their mistakes and taking responsibility for outcomes create a culture of accountability. When leaders set the example of self-reflection and continuous improvement, it signals to the team that everyone should take ownership of their roles and contributions.

Leaders' communication style, whether encouraging, critical, open, or closed, affects how team members interact. A leader who promotes open, respectful communication and listens actively encourages team members to share ideas and collaborate. Leaders who are dismissive or confrontational can create an atmosphere of fear or competition, hindering collaboration and open dialogue. Leaders who are passionate about their work and communicate the vision and mission of the organization inspire a sense of purpose in the team. When a leader believes in the team's goals and acts with integrity, it motivates others to align their efforts with the organization's objectives.

Ensure your attitude reflects the culture you want to create. Developing emotional intelligence is key to leading with the right attitude. Self-awareness helps leaders recognize their emotional responses and how those affect others. By managing stress, frustration, or uncertainty positively, leaders create a culture of resilience. Regular self-reflection and mindfulness practices can help leaders stay grounded and adjust their attitude when needed. Regularly assess how your mood and behavior impact the team, "Are you modeling patience and understanding?" "Are you reactive in stressful situations?" Develop practices like deep breathing or journaling to manage your emotions before engaging with the team.

Optimism is contagious; leaders who maintain a positive outlook, especially during difficult periods, help their teams focus on solutions rather than problems. By maintaining an optimistic attitude, leaders encourage the team to persevere, stay engaged, and believe in the possibility of success. In challenging moments, acknowledge difficulties but shift the focus to opportunities or solutions. Frame setbacks as learning experiences and express confidence in the team's ability to overcome them. Leaders should consistently embody the values they want their team to embrace, such as integrity, collaboration, innovation, or accountability. If you want to create a culture of innovation, show a willingness to take calculated risks and encourage your team to do the same. If transparency is a core value, ensure you are open about decisions and welcome feedback. Write down your organization's core values and reflect on how well your behavior aligns with them. Make a conscious effort to embody those values daily and lead by example.

Leaders who embrace a growth mindset inspire continuous team improvement and adaptability. This involves demonstrating a willingness to learn, accept feedback, and encourage experimentation. When leaders value learning and view challenges as opportunities, team members are likelier to take initiative, innovate, and embrace change. Share your learning experiences or failures with the team, showing that growth comes from success and setbacks. Encourage team members to take risks, knowing they won't be penalized for making mistakes as long as they learn from them. Empathy and listening to your team demonstrate that you value their input and concerns. Leaders who truly listen set a tone of respect, understanding, and openness. This leads to higher employee engagement, as team members feel their voices are heard and their contributions matter. Make it a habit to ask for feedback and listen without interrupting or being defensive. During conversations, focus on the speaker rather than planning your response. Acknowledge their perspective and provide thoughtful responses that reflect their concerns.

Leaders who consistently acknowledge and celebrate their teams' successes foster a culture of appreciation and motivation. Recognizing individual and team efforts encourages a sense of pride and reinforces the behaviors that contribute to success. Make recognition a regular part of your leadership practice, whether through public praise, personal notes of thanks, or celebrating team milestones. Ensure that your recognition is genuine and tailored to the individual's preferences.

Consistency in behavior and decision-making builds trust and credibility. Leaders who treat all team members fairly and uphold the same standards for everyone create a culture of equality and accountability. Inconsistencies, favoritism, or unpredictable behavior can erode trust and lead to disengagement. Regularly assess whether you consistently apply rules, rewards, and feedback across the team. Ensure that your behavior reflects fairness, even when making tough decisions. Leaders set the tone by actively participating in their team's day-to-day activities. A leader who is present, approachable, and engaged signals that they are invested in the team's success. Being available to support and guide your team shows you are committed to their well-being and growth. Make time for regular one-on-one meetings, team check-ins, and informal conversations. Show interest in your team member's personal and professional development by asking questions and offering support when needed.

Leaders who promote and demonstrate a healthy work-life balance encourage their team to do the same, preventing burnout and fostering long-term productivity. If you want to create a culture where well-being is prioritized, practice what you preach, whether taking time off, avoiding after-hours emails, or setting boundaries. Be transparent about your work-life balance practices, such as leaving work on time or prioritizing time with family. Encourage your team to take vacations and set boundaries between work and personal life.

A leader's attitude and behavior shape the work environment and directly influence team dynamics, productivity, and engagement. Leaders create a culture of trust, collaboration, and accountability by being self-aware, optimistic, and consistent. Strategies such as leading with optimism, embodying core values, practicing empathy, and recognizing achievements can ensure that a leader's attitude reflects the culture they want to build. Ultimately, leaders who model the behavior they wish to see set the tone for success, innovation, and well-being throughout the organization.

Chapter 10: Show the Way

Leading by example is the most powerful leadership tool to motivate your people. How leaders behave, embody their values, and lead by example are crucial in setting the tone for an organization's culture and success. Leaders who consistently demonstrate integrity, commitment, and empathy inspire trust and loyalty, creating a sense of purpose within their teams. When leaders live by the values they promote, they foster a culture of accountability, alignment, and motivation, making it easier for others to follow suit. These leaders don't just tell people what to do; they show how it's done, creating a powerful impact through their actions. When leaders practice what they preach, they earn the respect and trust of their teams. This credibility is essential for motivating and guiding others. Trust is the foundation of effective leadership; nothing undermines it more than leaders whose actions don't match their words.

You always want to reinforce organizational values, and leaders who embody the core values of their organization set the standard for others to follow. Whether it's accountability, innovation, or customer focus, leaders who consistently align with these values reinforce their importance across the organization. This also helps foster accountability; a leader's behavior creates an accountability model. When employees see leaders holding themselves to high standards, they are likelier to adopt the same level of responsibility and commitment in their roles. This helps create a culture of self-discipline and ownership. Leaders demonstrating empathy, respect, and transparency contribute to a healthy, positive work culture. This, in turn, fosters teamwork, open communication, and job satisfaction. People tend to mirror the behavior of those at the top, making the leader's actions highly influential in shaping the workplace environment. Leading by example is one of the most powerful ways to inspire others to act. When team members see their leaders working hard, making sacrifices, and facing challenges head-on, they are motivated to give their best. This leads to higher levels of engagement, loyalty, and overall performance.

Leaders committed to learning, self-improvement, and growth encourage their teams to adopt the same mindset. They show that striving for excellence is a journey and that setbacks or failures are learning opportunities. Mahatma Gandhi said, "Be the change you wish to see in the world." Gandhi is a prime example of a leader who lived by the values he promoted. His philosophy of nonviolent resistance, personal discipline, and self-sacrifice set a powerful example for millions. Gandhi's leadership during India's independence movement showed the world that leading by example can inspire profound societal change without violence. He didn't just advocate for peace; he lived it in his daily actions and decisions.

63

Nelson Mandela was an advocate for forgiveness and reconciliation. After spending 27 years in prison under South Africa's apartheid regime, Mandela emerged not with a desire for revenge but with a commitment to reconciliation. After his release, Mandela's leadership in uniting a divided nation was built on his personal values of forgiveness, equality, and justice. He led by example, creating policies and promoting dialogue that reflected these values, which ultimately helped dismantle apartheid and forge a new, democratic South Africa.

Howard Schultz, a former CEO of Starbucks, always promoted a "People-first" type of leadership. During his tenure at Starbucks, Schultz focused heavily on creating a company that valued its employees, referring to them as "partners." He famously ensured that Starbucks employees, even part-timers, received health care benefits and stock options. For example, Schultz's leadership put his employees' well-being at the forefront and built a company culture that thrived on collaboration and mutual respect. His values around equality, opportunity, and compassion were reflected in how he ran the business.

Jacinda Ardern, a New Zealand prime minister, led by empathy and authenticity. Ardern has been widely recognized for her empathetic leadership, especially during crises like the Christchurch terrorist attack and the COVID-19 pandemic. Ardern's transparent communication, compassionate decision-making, and ability to remain calm under pressure set her apart as a leader who embodies her values. She regularly demonstrated humility and care, listening to the needs of her citizens and responding with a sense of shared responsibility and humanity.

Captain Chesley "Sully" Sullenberger led by courage and accountability. Captain Sullenberger became an international hero after successfully landing a damaged airplane on the Hudson River in 2009, saving all 155 passengers. His calm and courageous response under pressure made him stand out, combined with years of preparation, discipline, and expertise. Sullenberger's dedication to safety and his sense of responsibility made him a role model for pilots and leaders in any field who must remain composed and accountable in critical moments.

Being a role model is important because it demonstrates the path forward. Leaders who act as role models provide a clear vision of what good behavior, hard work, and excellence look like in practice. When employees see their leaders doing the right thing, whether managing stress, working ethically, or leading with integrity, it sets a benchmark for others to follow. Role models don't just show what is possible; they encourage others to stretch their limits. A leader's actions can inspire team members to challenge themselves, develop new skills, and pursue excellence. Leaders who function as positive role models are inspiring through their actions along with the emotional and moral authority they carry. This influence goes beyond formal titles and job roles, as their personal integrity and commitment resonate more deeply with those around them. By being role models, leaders encourage others to learn and grow. When leaders admit their mistakes, show vulnerability, or are willing to learn, they promote a culture where continuous improvement and learning from failures are valued. This helps create a safe space for innovation and experimentation. As a role model, ensure that the team stays aligned with the organization's mission and values. By consistently demonstrating the behaviors they expect from others, role models help keep everyone on the same page, ensuring that individual actions contribute to shared goals. Role models inspire the next generation of leaders by setting a high standard. When aspiring leaders see the behaviors and qualities contributing to success, they are likelier to adopt those traits in their leadership journey.

Leading by example and embodying core values are foundational to effective leadership. Leaders who function as role models build trust, promote accountability and inspire higher levels of commitment from their teams. These leaders reinforce organizational values and set the tone for a positive culture by demonstrating empathy, integrity, and discipline. Iconic leaders like Gandhi, Mandela, Schultz, Ardern, and Captain Sully exemplify how living by one's values and actions can lead to transformational leadership. Their examples remind us that true leadership is not about commanding respect through words but earning it through consistent and authentic actions.

Chapter 11: Build Your Team

A leader's success is determined by their team; no one makes it alone. Creating a cohesive, high-performing team is essential for organizational success, as it drives productivity, innovation, and employee satisfaction. A well-functioning team can navigate challenges efficiently, communicate effectively, and deliver exceptional results. Major areas of building a team are recruitment, training, and fostering a positive culture. The foundation of a high-performing team begins with selecting the right individuals. When recruiting for your team, some metrics you should consider are skillset, culture fit, diversity, and growth potential. Ensuring that candidates have the necessary technical and soft skills to perform their roles effectively gives leaders confidence in their selection and a great base for their team. While current skills are crucial, recruiting for potential means bringing in people who are adaptable and eager to learn, which is critical for long-term success. Effective leaders also want to hire individuals who align with the company's values and vision. A team that shares similar core values tends to collaborate better. Another consideration is diversity; building a team with diverse backgrounds, perspectives, and experiences fosters creativity and innovation by bringing multiple viewpoints to problem-solving.

Even the most talented individuals need continual development to meet evolving business changes and needs. Effective training programs ensure that your team remains competitive and cohesive. Training should focus on skills, team building, and leadership development and explain your organization's feedback system. Skill development requires regular technical and soft skills training to help team members remain proficient in their roles and adapt to new challenges. A team is only as strong as its weakest link, so team building is as important as skill training. Leaders build up their teams through activities that strengthen communication, trust, and collaboration within the group. This helps individuals understand each other's working styles, strengths, and weaknesses. Many associate skilled technicians with leadership skills, and this is usually not the case. Being able to fix a mechanical issue doesn't use the same skills to fix leadership issues. Your best technicians might not be your best leader or manager option. This can be fixed by cultivating leadership skills within the team to ensure that individuals are empowered to take initiative, lead projects, and mentor others. All of these require feedback for continued growth. Feedback is often difficult for leaders to give or for your team to accept if not done effectively. Continuous feedback helps team members stay aligned with goals and expectations. Constructive criticism fosters improvement, while praise reinforces positive behaviors.

A positive work culture is essential to sustaining high performance over time. It helps create an environment where team members are motivated, engaged, and committed to their roles. Key aspects include open communication, recognition, psychological safety, work-life balance, and inclusivity. Establishing clear, transparent lines of communication encourages trust, prevents misunderstandings, and fosters collaboration. Recognition and rewards help in acknowledging accomplishments. Providing incentives boosts morale and motivates individuals to maintain high performance. Team members need to feel comfortable voicing opinions, asking questions, and taking risks without fear of retribution; this encourages creativity and innovation. Promoting well-being and preventing burnout ensures that employees remain productive and engaged over the long term. Creating an environment where everyone feels valued, fosters collaboration and loyalty, leads to better team cohesion. Building a cohesive, high-performing team requires intentional efforts in recruitment, training, and nurturing a positive organizational culture. Organizations can unlock their team's full potential by focusing on these areas, driving sustained performance and success.

You must also continuously develop your team. Developing others is a key leadership responsibility; identifying, nurturing, and managing talent is critical to organizational success. The ability to attract, develop, and retain skilled individuals is essential for driving innovation, achieving long-term goals, and maintaining a competitive edge. Effective talent management boosts performance and prepares the organization for future challenges. Succession planning and career development are key elements within this framework, ensuring continuity and fostering employee growth. High-performing employees drive productivity and innovation. Identifying and nurturing top talent ensures that the organization operates at its full potential and can meet its goals effectively. Managing talent well helps reduce turnover by making employees feel valued, supported, and aligned with the organization's vision. Talented individuals are likelier to stay when they see a clear career path and growth opportunities.

Talent management includes developing future leaders. By nurturing leadership potential within the organization, companies ensure they are prepared for future challenges and avoid disruptions caused by leadership gaps. Effective talent management creates an environment where employees feel motivated, engaged, and invested. This positive culture contributes to higher job satisfaction and team cohesion, enhancing overall organizational health. The right talent is critical for adapting to change, staying competitive, and fostering a culture of continuous improvement. Identifying and developing individuals with innovative ideas and the ability to adapt ensures the organization stays relevant in a dynamic, ever-changing market.

Effective leaders will continuously assess skills and competencies. Use performance reviews, feedback from peers and supervisors, and self-assessments to identify high-potential employees. Look for technical skills, leadership potential, creativity, and problem-solving abilities. Tools like personality assessments, cognitive tests, and behavioral interviews can provide deeper insights into an employee's strengths, potential, and fit within leadership roles. Gathering input from various sources, such as managers, peers, and direct reports, offers a holistic view of an employee's performance, leadership potential, and interpersonal skills.

Leaders also provide a means for training and development. Provide employees continuous learning opportunities through workshops, seminars, and certifications that enhance their skills and prepare them for future roles. Pairing high-potential employees with experienced mentors or coaches helps them develop leadership skills, gain industry insights, and navigate career challenges. Mentoring builds confidence and guides individuals toward growth opportunities. Offer employees stretch assignments that push them beyond their comfort zones. This allows them to gain new experiences, take calculated risks, and grow in areas where they show potential. Regular feedback helps employees understand their strengths and areas for improvement. Constructive feedback helps employees develop and advance in their careers when coupled with support and resources.

Establish clear goals and metrics to evaluate employee performance and identify high achievers. Use data-driven approaches to track progress and make informed decisions about

71

promotions and development opportunities. Keeping employees engaged is critical for managing talent effectively. Regular check-ins, recognition programs, and career path discussions ensure employees feel valued and motivated to stay with the organization.

A diverse talent pool brings varied perspectives and ideas, enhancing creativity and problem-solving. Make talent management inclusive by identifying and nurturing talent from all backgrounds and creating opportunities for everyone to thrive. Building a succession plan is a great way to ensure continued success. Succession planning is a proactive process to ensure that key roles within an organization are filled by qualified individuals when current leaders retire, leave, or move into new roles. This prepares organizations for planned and unplanned leadership changes and ensures business continuity. A well-structured succession plan ensures no leadership vacuum or single point of failure, allowing the organization to transition smoothly during times of change. Succession planning mitigates the risks associated with sudden departures of key personnel by ensuring that successors are ready to step into critical roles.

Grooming internal candidates for leadership roles helps retain valuable institutional knowledge, ensuring that expertise is passed down and not lost when leaders move on. When employees see that the organization is committed to long-term growth and offers leadership opportunities, they are likelier to remain loyal and engaged.

Succession planning is critical for longevity; identifying key positions within the organization increases the likelihood of the organization's success. These roles are not limited to executive positions but can include key technical, operational, or strategic roles. Use performance data, assessments, and leadership potential evaluations to identify employees who could step into critical roles. Look for individuals who demonstrate leadership qualities, adaptability, and a strong understanding of the business. For each potential successor, create a development plan that outlines the skills, experiences, and training they need to be ready for the role. This might include mentoring, job rotations, or leadership training programs. Allow high-potential employees to work in different departments or on diverse projects. This cross-training helps them understand the organization better and prepares them for leadership roles. Succession planning should be an ongoing process. Review and update the plan regularly to account for organizational strategic direction changes, employee performance, and career development.

Career development is how employees enhance their skills, advance their careers, and reach their professional goals within the organization. Organizations benefit from offering career development opportunities as it helps retain top talent, boost employee satisfaction, and improve overall organizational performance. Employees are more likely to stay with organizations that invest in their growth and provide opportunities for advancement. Career development programs allow employees to upgrade their skills, making them more effective in their current roles and preparing them for future opportunities. Employees who see a clear path for advancement and personal growth are more motivated and engaged in their work. Career development ensures a steady pipeline of employees ready to move into leadership roles when needed. Create Individual Development Plans (IDPs) for your employees. Leaders should work with employees to create personalized development plans that outline their career goals, and the steps needed to achieve them. IDPs should include skills training, mentorship, and stretch assignments that align with their ambitions. Also, it offers learning and development opportunities by providing access to training programs, courses, and certifications that help employees build the skills they need for future roles. Encourage lifelong learning and continuous improvement. Promote internal job opportunities to encourage employees to move across departments or take on new organizational roles. This not only fosters growth but also keeps talented employees within the company. Pair employees with mentors or coaches who can provide guidance, share experiences, and offer support in their career development journey. This helps employees develop both soft and technical skills. Acknowledge employees who actively pursue career development and show progress. Offering a promotion, raise, or new responsibilities as a reward for their growth will encourage others to take their development seriously.

Identifying, nurturing, and managing talent is essential for building a high-performing organization that is prepared for the future. By focusing on succession planning and career development, leaders can ensure continuity, build a strong leadership pipeline, and keep employees engaged and motivated. Mentoring, training, feedback, and regular assessments help foster growth and align employees with the organization's long-term vision. Investing in talent management and development is crucial for individual success and organizational resilience and sustainability.

Chapter 12: Mentorship

Mentoring is an influential tool for personal and professional growth, benefiting both the mentor and the mentee. It facilitates the transfer of knowledge, skills, and wisdom while fostering mutual growth and development. Whether in leadership, business, or personal development, mentoring relationships create pathways for learning, self-reflection, and progress. Mentoring allows leaders to cultivate the next generation of talent, ensuring the continuity of knowledge and experience. By mentoring others, leaders help mentees develop critical skills, from problem-solving to decision-making, which equips them to handle future challenges. Additionally, mentoring is a key component of servant leadership. Leaders who focus on the growth and well-being of others contribute to a healthier, more productive organizational culture. Bill Gates has often cited Warren Buffett as a mentor from whom he learned about strategic decision-making and philanthropy. By passing down insights, Buffett shaped Gates' professional trajectory and influenced his approach to global issues.

Mentoring is a two-way street; mentors offer guidance and learn from their mentees' fresh perspectives, insights, and ideas. This exchange can stimulate both parties' new ways of thinking and problem-solving, especially in rapidly evolving fields such as technology or entrepreneurship. In reverse mentoring programs, younger employees often mentor older executives on technology or trends like social media, helping leaders stay relevant in a fast-paced digital world. This dynamic keeps leaders informed while offering younger professionals growth opportunities.

Mentoring allows experienced individuals to leave a legacy by positively influencing others' careers or lives. It's a way to give back to the community, ensuring that the knowledge and experience accumulated over the years don't remain siloed but enrich the future generation. Through mentoring, one's influence extends beyond their direct work. Oprah Winfrey, who Maya Angelou mentored, has often spoken about how mentorship shaped her career and life. Now, Oprah has become a mentor, creating a ripple effect that impacts many.

Mentoring provides access to a wealth of experience and expertise, allowing mentees to learn faster than they would alone. A mentor helps navigate challenges, avoid common mistakes, and focus on key areas of development. This guidance is invaluable, particularly for those at the start of their career or entering new fields. Sheryl Sandberg, COO of Facebook, was mentored by Larry Summers during her time at the U.S. Treasury. This relationship provided her with critical insights into leadership and management that shaped her career and helped her rise to the top of the tech industry. A mentor offers a fresh, objective perspective, often identifying areas for improvement or opportunities that may not be immediately obvious to the mentee. Constructive feedback from a trusted mentor helps mentees refine their skills, improve their strategies, and grow in self-awareness. During his early career, Steve Jobs mentored Mark Zuckerberg, who provided guidance on leadership and vision, helping Zuckerberg navigate the growing pains of building Facebook.

Mentorship also provides emotional support, especially during challenging times. Having a mentor to turn to when facing difficult decisions or setbacks helps build confidence and resilience. Mentors often provide encouragement and validation, which can be instrumental in overcoming self-doubt or imposter syndrome. Throughout her career, Indra Nooyi, former CEO of PepsiCo, received guidance from several mentors who helped her navigate cultural and gender biases in the corporate world, providing professional advice and personal encouragement.

Before seeking a mentor, clarify what you want to achieve. Are you seeking career advice, skill development, or guidance on a particular challenge? Having clear goals helps you find the right mentor and ensures your relationship remains focused and productive. Reflect on your strengths and weaknesses to determine what areas you want to grow in and seek a mentor with that particular experience or expertise. Don't wait for a mentor to find you; take the initiative to reach out to potential mentors, whether within your organization or externally. Approach them respectfully and express your desire to learn from their experience, clarifying why you value their guidance. When reaching out, highlight your goals and how you believe the mentor can help. Show appreciation for their time and make your request clear and concise.

A key aspect of being mentored is being open to constructive criticism. Mentors will often challenge you to think differently or improve in areas you might not have recognized as weaknesses. Be willing to listen and act on their advice. After receiving feedback, reflect on it and put it into action. Following up with your mentor on how you applied their advice demonstrates your commitment and growth. Mentors are often very busy with limited time; be respectful of their schedule by preparing for meetings, keeping them concise, and only requesting their time when necessary. Come to each encounter with specific questions or topics to discuss, showing that you value their time. Set a regular meeting schedule, such as monthly or quarterly, and be flexible if your mentor's availability changes. Always express gratitude for their time and guidance.

One of the most important aspects of being a mentor is listening. Understand your mentee's goals, concerns, and challenges before offering advice. Sometimes, mentees just need a sounding board to help them articulate their thoughts. Ask open-ended questions encouraging your mentee to think critically about their goals and decisions. Listening carefully helps you offer more tailored and effective guidance. Offer specific, actionable advice rather than abstract suggestions. Help your mentee break down big goals into smaller, achievable steps; this guidance empowers mentees to take meaningful actions and track their progress. Share relevant stories from your own experience, including challenges you faced and how you overcame them. This practical wisdom can provide valuable context for the mentee.

While mentors offer guidance, it's important not to micromanage or dictate the mentee's decisions. Instead, encourage them to think critically and make their own choices. The goal of mentorship is to develop their independence and leadership skills. Ask your mentee what they think the best course of action is before offering your perspective. Help them explore different options and weigh the pros and cons to build decision-making confidence. Celebrate your mentee's successes and offer encouragement when they achieve milestones. When things don't go as planned, use those moments as opportunities to teach resilience and reflection. After a setback, help your mentee analyze what went wrong and what could be done differently next time. This turns failure into a learning experience and builds resilience.

Mentorship is a dynamic relationship that fosters growth, development, and mutual learning. By mentoring others, leaders leave a lasting legacy and sharpen their skills, while being mentored accelerates personal and professional growth. To establish and maintain effective mentoring relationships, mentors and mentees must communicate openly, respect each other's time, and focus on growth. A successful mentoring relationship helps individuals reach their potential and strengthens teams and organizations through shared wisdom and mutual support.

Chapter 13: Say Less, Listen More

Active listening is a leader's secret weapon. Effective leaders understand the power of listening, often valuing it more than speaking. By actively listening to their team members, they gain insights into ideas, concerns, and perspectives that might be overlooked. This helps make better-informed decisions, builds trust, fosters open communication, and creates an environment where people feel heard and valued. Leaders who listen well are better equipped to identify challenges early, uncover hidden opportunities, and encourage collaboration.

There's an old saying that you have two ears and one mouth, so you should listen twice as much as you speak. Leaders who listen more than they speak gain deeper insights into the organization's dynamics, employee concerns, and workplace environment. Active listening helps leaders understand the real issues beyond surface-level feedback, enabling more thoughtful decision-making. Listening attentively shows that leaders care about what others have to say, which builds trust and fosters stronger relationships. When employees feel heard, they are likelier to be honest, transparent, and engaged, creating a culture of openness.

Listening more effectively creates space for different perspectives, encouraging creativity and innovation. This helps the team feel more invested in outcomes, knowing their ideas are taken seriously. This allows you to gather various inputs before making decisions; leaders can weigh different perspectives and gather valuable information. This results in more thoughtful, balanced decisions that consider the organization's and its employees' needs. Employees who feel their voices are heard are more engaged, motivated, and loyal. Effective listening creates a feedback loop where employees are more likely to share insights, knowing their input is valued, leading to a more positive and productive work environment.

Active listening is a key communication component and involves fully focusing on the speaker, acknowledging their message, and responding thoughtfully. Leaders should avoid distractions like checking emails or thinking about their responses while someone is speaking. Instead, they should maintain eye contact, use nonverbal and verbal cues like nodding to show understanding, and "I see" or "That's a good point." This demonstrates genuine engagement with the speaker. You should also take a moment to process what was said before responding rather than jumping in with a solution or opinion. In many cases, before the speaker is done speaking, we have already started to formulate a response or have the response before they are done speaking. To help combat this, encourage the speaker to share more by asking open-ended questions. This helps leaders dig deeper into issues and gather more comprehensive insights. Open-ended questions like "Can you tell me more about that?" or "What are your thoughts on this approach?" prompt detailed responses and encourage dialogue. Try to avoid "yes" and "no" questions; instead, use questions that start with "how," "what," or "why" to explore topics in more depth. Silence can be an effective tool in conversations. Giving the speaker time to reflect and elaborate without rushing to fill gaps shows patience and thoughtfulness. Silence allows people to gather their thoughts and often leads to more in-depth discussions. After someone finishes speaking, take a brief pause before responding. This encourages the other person to continue if they have more to share.

Paraphrasing and summarizing what the speaker said helps ensure the leader fully understands the message. By repeating key points in their own words, leaders confirm their understanding and show they are paying close attention. To verify you understand completely what is being asked, after someone shares an idea or concern, say something like, "So if I understand correctly, you're saying that…" This ensures clarity and avoids misunderstandings.

Listening isn't just about the words being spoken; it also involves paying attention to nonverbal cues like body language, tone of voice, and facial expressions. Leaders attuned to these signals can often notice unspoken concerns or emotions. Effective leaders watch for changes in body language, such as crossed arms or a shift in tone, which may indicate discomfort, hesitation, or stress. Address

84

these cues by asking follow-up questions to clarify what the person may not be saying explicitly. Resist the temptation to interrupt or immediately jump in with solutions. Instead, let the speaker finish, encouraging them to share more and think more deeply about the issue. This also avoids cutting off important insights. Instead of offering solutions immediately, ask the person, "How do you think we should approach this?" This encourages problem-solving and empowers the speaker to contribute to the solution. Sometimes, what a person says may not fully capture their feelings. Leaders who are empathetic listeners can notice the emotional aspects and provide support accordingly. Understanding non-verbal communication, such as emotions like frustration, excitement, or anxiety, helps leaders address the root causes of issues. If someone seems emotional or stressed, acknowledge it with statements like, "I can see this is important to you" or "It sounds like this situation has been challenging." This creates an empathetic space for the speaker to open up.

After listening carefully, leaders can offer constructive feedback or ask clarifying questions to deepen the conversation. Feedback should focus on validating the speaker's input while offering thoughts or suggestions, encouraging further dialogue. Attempt to always use positive reinforcement, such as "I appreciate your perspective on this," before offering any critiques or suggestions. This helps build confidence and maintain a positive rapport.

Listening doesn't stop when the conversation ends. Effective leaders follow up on shared concerns, ideas, or feedback. This could involve acting on specific requests, addressing concerns, or simply checking in to see how things are progressing. By following through, leaders demonstrate that they value what was shared and are committed to acting on it. After a conversation, send a follow-up email or set a reminder to revisit the topic in the next meeting. This reinforces that the conversation is important, and that the leader is accountable.

Leaders who actively listen foster a culture where employees feel comfortable sharing their thoughts and ideas. Regularly scheduling one-on-ones, hosting open forums, and encouraging feedback create a culture of transparency and openness. Set up anonymous feedback channels for team members who may be more reserved or hesitant to speak openly in public settings.

Effective leadership involves listening more than speaking. Leaders who actively listen, ask open-ended questions, and provide thoughtful feedback gain better insights into their teams and make more informed decisions. Listening builds trust, enhances collaboration, and increases employee engagement. By using strategies such as active listening, paraphrasing, embracing silence, and recognizing emotional cues, leaders can create a work environment where communication is open, employees feel valued, and decisions are made with a full understanding of the situation.

Chapter 14: Leave Emotion Out of It

Emotional control is essential for effective leadership; leaders must manage their emotions. In high-stakes situations, effective leadership hinges on technical expertise, decision-making skills, and managing emotions. Leaders are often in the spotlight, and how they handle their emotions can set the tone for the entire team. Emotional intelligence and self-regulation are critical components of effective leadership, especially when high-stress and significant stakes are present. When leaders can manage their emotions, they inspire confidence, maintain focus, and guide their teams through challenges with resilience and composure. Leaders function as emotional barometers for their teams. If a leader is calm and collected, it can help stabilize the team and foster an atmosphere of rational decision-making. Conversely, a leader who reacts impulsively or shows signs of stress can spread anxiety and confusion. High-stakes situations often demand clear, rational thinking, and emotional overload can cloud judgment, leading to hasty or ill-considered decisions. Leaders who regulate their emotions can better focus on the facts, assess risks, and make sound decisions under pressure. Emotional outbursts or unchecked frustration can damage relationships, erode trust, and diminish a leader's credibility. In contrast, leaders who manage their emotions foster respect, even in difficult conversations or crises.

Managing emotions is essential not only for leading others but also for personal well-being. Constant stress without emotional regulation can lead to burnout, poor health, and diminished effectiveness. The foundation of emotional intelligence is the ability to recognize and understand your own emotions. Self-aware leaders can better identify when their emotions are rising and take steps to manage them before they influence behavior. This is the ability to control or redirect disruptive emotions and impulses. In high-stakes situations, self-regulation helps leaders avoid reacting in ways they might later regret, such as losing their temper or making emotional decisions. Understanding and considering the emotions of others is crucial in leadership. In stressful situations, showing empathy can help leaders connect with their team, understand their concerns, and provide support to keep morale high.

Emotionally intelligent leaders are driven by internal motivations, such as the desire to achieve and grow, rather than being reactive to external pressures. This enables them to focus on long-term goals, even in challenging circumstances. Effective leaders use their emotional intelligence to build strong relationships, communicate clearly, and inspire collaboration, even in difficult times. These social skills help leaders navigate conflicts, manage team dynamics, and maintain morale.

In high-stress or intense situations, pause, breathe deeply, and gather your thoughts before responding. This simple act of mindfulness can prevent emotional reactivity. By pausing, leaders allow themselves to process emotions, assess the situation objectively, and choose a response that aligns with their long-term goals rather than reacting impulsively. Reframing the situation is a cognitive strategy that helps leaders see the situation from a different perspective. Instead of viewing a high-stakes challenge as a threat, leaders can reframe it as an opportunity for growth, innovation, or learning. This shift in mindset reduces stress and enables a more constructive response, focusing on solutions rather than problems.

In high-pressure scenarios, it's easy to become overwhelmed by factors outside your control. Effective leaders concentrate on what they can control, such as their behavior, communication, and the immediate next steps. This helps reduce feelings of helplessness and allows for actionable problem-solving, which also has a calming effect on the leader and resonates within the team. Realizing and using emotional triggers as data and understanding emotions, especially negative ones like anger or frustration, can help leaders act against these impulses. However, they can also provide valuable data about underlying issues or stressors. Emotionally intelligent leaders don't suppress their feelings; they analyze them. When experiencing strong emotions, ask yourself, "Why am I feeling this way?" or "What triggered this?" This introspection can help resolve the root cause of stress and improve decision-making.

Identifying these triggers can help you establish personal practices that help create emotional buffer zones, such as regular physical exercise, meditation, or hobbies that allow leaders to decompress. These practices can help regulate emotions and prevent stress from escalating to unmanageable levels. Scheduling regular breaks, taking time to reflect, and maintaining a work-life balance are also important for long-term emotional regulation.

In stressful situations, sometimes, the less you say, the more you understand. Leaders should prioritize listening over speaking. Active listening helps leaders better understand the concerns and emotions of others, which can prevent misunderstandings and help de-escalate tense situations. When leaders listen without rushing to respond, they show empathy and consideration, which fosters trust and keeps the team united in the face of challenges.

Emotions can cloud even the most self-aware leaders; find someone you can benefit from by seeking an outside perspective. Trusted mentors, peers, or coaches can provide feedback on how a leader's emotions affect their decisions and behavior. Sharing challenges with a trusted colleague can also be a safe outlet for emotions, reducing the risk of overreacting or taking stress out on the team.

Leaders should prepare for high-stakes situations by visualizing how to handle the situation calmly and effectively. Leaders build confidence and emotional resilience by mentally rehearsing potential challenges and visualizing successful outcomes. This technique can help reduce anxiety and increase preparedness when facing real-world stressors. Being honest about emotions, within reason, can build trust and help others feel more comfortable managing their emotions. For example, acknowledging, "This is a stressful situation, but we're going to work through it together," shows authenticity without losing control. This transparency allows leaders to connect with their team emotionally while demonstrating control and confidence.

In high-stakes situations, managing emotions is a critical leadership skill. Leaders with high emotional intelligence and self-regulation inspire confidence, maintain focus, and help their teams navigate challenges with resilience. Strategies such as mindfulness, reframing, focusing on controllable factors, active listening, and seeking support all help leaders stay composed and make better decisions under pressure. By mastering their emotions, leaders enhance their personal effectiveness and build a culture of trust, collaboration, and stability within their teams.

Chapter 15: Seek Intelligence

Effective leaders understand intelligence is an asset, not a threat. Great leaders realize that their success depends not solely on their intelligence or abilities but on their ability to surround themselves with smart, capable people and leverage their expertise. Elon Musk said, "Don't confuse schooling with education. I didn't go to Harvard but the people that work for me did." By building a team of talented individuals and empowering them to use their skills, leaders can amplify the impact of the entire organization. This requires creating an environment where intelligent team members feel valued, trusted, and empowered to contribute their insights and ideas.

No leader can be an expert in every field; by surrounding themselves with people who bring diverse perspectives and specialized expertise, leaders can tap into a broader range of solutions, creativity, and innovation. The team's collective intelligence enables the leader to make better-informed decisions and address challenges from multiple angles. Steve Jobs of Apple was known for surrounding himself with incredibly talented people who were known experts in their fields. Jobs' ability to tap into his team's expertise while providing a vision for the company allowed Apple to create revolutionary products.

Every leader has strengths and weaknesses, and by surrounding yourself with intelligent people, you ensure that the strengths of others cover your weaknesses. This complementarity creates a more balanced and effective leadership approach. President Abraham Lincoln built a "team of rivals" by appointing people with differing views and expertise to his cabinet. He understood that surrounding himself with intelligent, sometimes opposing voices would make him a stronger leader, helping him navigate the complexities of leading the country through the Civil War.

Intelligent people are often curious, creative, and driven to innovate. By empowering them, leaders create an environment where ideas can flourish, leading to breakthroughs and continuous improvement. When team members feel their intelligence is valued, they are more likely to take risks and pursue new opportunities. Google's founders, Larry Page and Sergey Brin, prioritized hiring highly intelligent and creative people. They fostered an environment where innovation was encouraged, leading to groundbreaking products like Gmail, Google Maps, and Android. Leaders who surround themselves with intelligent people gain the ability to trust and delegate responsibilities effectively. This frees the leader to focus on strategic vision and higher-level decision-making while trusting their team to handle the details. It also helps develop the next generation of leaders within the organization. Warren Buffett is known for hiring smart managers and giving them a high degree of autonomy to run their businesses. Buffett's trust in the expertise of his team allows him to focus on the broader strategy of Berkshire Hathaway without micromanaging each business unit.

Challenge and empower intelligent team members and create an environment where they feel encouraged to share their ideas, even if they go against the norm. Open communication and collaboration are essential for leveraging the team's collective intelligence. Leaders should listen actively and be open to feedback and suggestions from all levels of the organization. Hold regular brainstorming sessions, promote cross-functional collaboration, and create channels where employees can openly share their insights. Encourage team members to bring diverse perspectives and solutions and clarify that all voices are valued. Reed Hastings, CEO of Netflix, encourages a culture of candid feedback, where employees are empowered to speak up and challenge ideas, including those of leadership. This culture of openness helps Netflix remain agile and innovative in a fast-changing industry.

Empower intelligence by giving them ownership of important projects and decisions. This shows that you trust their judgment and believe in their abilities. Leaders who delegate effectively create opportunities for team members to demonstrate their expertise and grow within the organization. Assign key projects to team members based on their strengths and expertise and give them the autonomy to execute their vision. Avoid micromanaging but provide support when needed to ensure they have the resources and guidance to succeed. When Eric Schmidt was hired as CEO of Google, he delegated many day-to-day decisions to senior executives, allowing them to focus on their specific areas of expertise. This empowered executives like Marissa Mayer and Sundar Pichai to lead major initiatives, contributing to Google's overall success.

Recognize and reward contributions; intelligent team members need to feel that their contributions are recognized and valued. By publicly acknowledging their achievements, leaders reinforce the importance of their work and motivate them to continue striving for excellence. This also sets a standard for other team members, encouraging a culture that strives for excellence. Celebrate individual and team successes regularly, privately and publicly, by offering promotions, bonuses, or opportunities for further growth to high-performing team members. Recognition can also come in giving credit where it's due, ensuring that team members' contributions are visible to the organization. Sheryl Sandberg, former COO of Facebook, was known for recognizing the contributions of her team and crediting them for their work in public forums. This helped create a culture of appreciation and collaboration, where employees felt their efforts were acknowledged.

Invest in employee development; their success is your success! Smart people thrive in environments that challenge them and offer growth opportunities. Leaders can empower their teams by investing in professional development through training, mentorship, or opportunities for advancement. This improves their skills and increases their loyalty and engagement with the organization.

Provide ongoing training, access to industry conferences, and opportunities for team members to expand their skill sets. Offer mentorship and create pathways for career progression to ensure that your smartest employees feel they are continually growing. Under Jack Welch, a major focus was placed on leadership development at General Electrics. GE invested heavily in training and mentorship programs, ensuring talented employees were constantly improving and being groomed for leadership roles.

Intelligent people often develop bold, innovative ideas that carry a degree of risk. Empowering them means allowing them to experiment and, if necessary, fail without fear of punishment. Leaders who foster a safe environment for taking risks enable their team members to push boundaries and explore new solutions. Encourage experimentation by creating pilot projects or initiatives where team members can try out new ideas in a low-risk setting. When failures occur, use them as learning opportunities rather than assigning blame. Amazon encourages employees to take risks and experiment with innovative ideas, as demonstrated by their willingness to embrace failure as part of the innovation process. Jeff Bezos has often spoken about how the company's biggest successes, like AWS and Kindle, came from teams willing to take calculated risks and learn from their mistakes.

While intelligent team members may be highly capable, they still need a clear vision and direction to channel their efforts effectively. Leaders must provide a compelling vision of where the organization is headed and align their team's work with that vision. This helps

96

them understand how their contributions fit the bigger picture and motivates them to excel. Regularly communicate the organization's vision and strategic goals and show team members how their work directly contributes to achieving them. Ensure that individual and team goals are aligned with the organization's broader objectives. Elon Musk is known for setting ambitious, visionary goals for his companies, such as Tesla's mission to accelerate the world's transition to sustainable energy. By clearly articulating this vision, Musk inspires his team to work toward bold, challenging goals while leveraging their expertise to make it a reality.

Great leaders understand that they cannot succeed in isolation. Surrounding themselves with intelligent, capable people and leveraging their expertise is essential to driving innovation, solving complex problems, and achieving organizational goals. By fostering an environment of collaboration, trust, and empowerment, leaders can maximize the potential of their team members while developing future leaders. The most successful leaders, like Jobs, Bezos, and Sandberg, have demonstrated that empowering intelligent people benefits the organization and creates a culture of excellence and innovation.

Chapter 16: Vision with a Plan

Vision gives direction and purpose; crafting and communicating a compelling vision are leaders' most powerful tools to inspire and align teams. A clear, well-articulated vision provides direction, purpose, and motivation. It helps team members understand the bigger picture and rally around a common goal, fostering unity and high performance. Leaders must understand the purpose or vision before communicating it to their people. The vision should reflect the purpose of the organization or team. Leaders should clearly define why the team exists and what impact they seek to make. This ensures the vision has deep meaning, resonating with and inspiring people. For example, John F Kennedy's vision to put a man on the moon was not just a technological goal but a statement of national purpose in advancing human progress and asserting leadership in the space race.

A vision must be easily understood and visualized. It should be specific enough that team members can grasp the desired future. Ambiguity can diminish inspiration; take Martin Luther King Jr.'s "I Have a Dream" speech. His vision of racial equality was expressed in simple yet profound terms, making it relatable to people across generations and societal backgrounds. A great vision should be ambitious enough to inspire yet grounded enough that people believe it's possible. Stretching people beyond their comfort zones motivates them to grow, but the vision must be attainable to avoid discouragement. Elon Musk, for example, set an ambitious vision to revolutionize transportation with electric vehicles through Tesla and to explore space colonization through SpaceX. While bold, his vision is supported by clear, incremental steps that make progress toward these goals feel achievable.

A vision resonates most when it aligns with the values of the people involved. Leaders should identify the core values of their teams and ensure the vision reflects those values. For example, Howard Schultz, the former CEO of Starbucks, communicated a vision of creating a company that sold coffee and built a community. This vision aligned with Starbucks' core values of connection and inclusivity, motivating employees to deliver more than just a product but an experience. Humans connect emotionally with stories, and a compelling vision is best communicated through storytelling. Visionary leaders often use personal anecdotes, historical references, or metaphors to make the vision relatable. Steve Jobs was an expert in storytelling, often weaving narratives about how Apple products would change technology and fundamentally improve lives, connecting employees and customers to a larger cause. A vision must be communicated often and in different formats; repetition is key to embedding it into the team's mindset. Leaders should share the vision during meetings, one-on-one conversations, company updates, and written communication. Walt Disney famously repeated his vision of creating "the happiest place on Earth" to his employees. His persistent and clear communication of this idea inspired generations of employees to live up to the company's mission.

Visionary leaders don't just announce their vision; they invite others to take ownership of it. This means creating opportunities for team members to contribute their ideas and be part of the journey toward achieving the vision. Employees who feel a sense of ownership are more committed to the vision. Nelson Mandela, for example, engaged his team in the fight against apartheid by showing people how their efforts contributed to the broader vision of a free and equal South Africa. He inspired collective ownership, which strengthened the movement. Visionary leaders constantly tie the vision back to daily tasks and goals to sustain momentum. Leaders should show how each team member's work contributes to achieving the broader vision, directly linking what people do each day and the larger purpose. For instance, at Amazon, Jeff Bezos consistently ties the vision of being "the most customer-centric company" to every employee's role, encouraging even small daily actions to improve the customer experience.

Going back to President Kennedy, in 1961, he set the vision for the United States to land a man on the moon by the decade's end. His clear, ambitious goal inspired a generation of scientists, engineers, and astronauts and aligned thousands of people across

NASA and government agencies. This led to the successful Apollo 11 mission in 1969. Steve Jobs is another example of having a vision. As the visionary leader of Apple, Jobs had a clear vision of creating technology that was functional, aesthetically pleasing, and easy to use. He consistently communicated this vision, leading to groundbreaking innovations like the iPhone and iMac and aligning the company around simplicity and design excellence. Nelson Mandela's vision of a united, democratic South Africa, free from apartheid, inspired millions. Despite extreme adversity, he consistently communicated his message of reconciliation and equality, uniting oppressed and oppressors to work toward a peaceful transition of power. Elon Musk's vision of advancing humanity to become a multi-planetary species through SpaceX while driving sustainable energy solutions through Tesla has rallied teams around ambitious goals. His relentless pursuit of these visionary objectives has inspired groundbreaking achievements in space exploration and electric vehicles.

Crafting and communicating a vision that inspires teams is an essential leadership skill. The vision must be clear, ambitious, values-aligned, and relatable to the team's daily work. Visionary leaders such as Kennedy, Jobs, and Musk have shown how a powerful vision can unite and propel teams toward extraordinary achievements. By consistently communicating the vision and engaging people in its pursuit, leaders can align their teams around a common goal, fostering motivation, commitment, and high performance.

Effective leaders strategize and plan for success. Creating actionable, strategic plans is vital for guiding an organization or team toward achieving long-term objectives. Effective strategic planning involves defining the overall direction and developing specific, actionable steps that ensure progress. Incorporating structured frameworks like SWOT (Strengths, Weaknesses, Opportunities, and Threats) analysis and SMART goals into this process can help create clarity and ensure the plan is practical and achievable. Before developing any strategic plan, it's important to define the overarching goals. This is often linked to the organization's mission and vision. These objectives guide the planning process by determining where the organization wants to go. Conducting a comprehensive situation analysis can help this process. A thorough understanding of the internal and external environment is crucial. This includes analyzing the organization's strengths and weaknesses as well as the opportunities and threats in the market or industry. This can be effectively structured using the SWOT analysis, a widely used framework for strategic planning. It provides a structured way to assess internal and external factors that could impact the strategic plan's success. Understanding and knowing an organization's strengths, weaknesses, opportunities, and threats assist in developing a successful plan.

Leaders can dissect what their organization does well, knowing what resources, capabilities, or assets give it a competitive edge. For example, a company might have strong brand recognition or an innovative product line. This can also help identify internal factors that could hinder progress. These could include a lack of financial resources, poor processes, or talent gaps. Also, understanding what external factors the organization can leverage for growth is valuable information for effective leaders. This could be market expansion, technological advancements, or changes in consumer behavior. Leaders also need to examine external risks that could negatively affect the organization. Threats may include new competitors, regulatory changes, or economic downturns. Using SWOT analysis, leaders can identify key focus areas and prioritize initiatives that capitalize on strengths and opportunities while addressing weaknesses and mitigating threats.

Once the SWOT analysis has formed the broader strategic direction, the next step is to create specific, actionable goals. The SMART goals framework effectively ensures that goals are clear and achievable. Clearly define what needs to be achieved. The goal should be precise, leaving no room for ambiguity. For example, instead of saying "increase productivity," a specific goal would be "increase productivity by 15% in the next quarter." These goals must be measurable and track progress. There should be clear metrics to evaluate success; tracking weekly sales reports, customer acquisition numbers, or employee performance can make the goal measurable. The goal must be realistic and attainable, considering the organization's current resources, capabilities, and constraints. It's important to challenge the team without setting them up for failure. Leaders must ensure the goal is aligned with the broader strategic objectives. Every goal should contribute to the long-term vision of

103

the organization or team. Finally, for a plan to be effective, set a specific deadline or timeline for achieving the goal. This creates urgency and a sense of accountability. For example, "complete the new product launch within six months." Once goals are established using the SMART framework, breaking them down into actionable steps ensures the plan is manageable and trackable. Each goal should have an action plan with key milestones, responsibilities, resources, and progress. Break the goal into smaller milestones or phases, each with its deadlines. Clearly define who is responsible for each action step or milestone. Accountability is key to ensuring that tasks are completed on time and correctly. Ensure that the necessary resources, such as budget, personnel, and tools, are available to support the action steps. Regularly review progress toward goals, adjust the plan as needed, and address challenges that arise.

This strategic planning tool helps organizations link objectives to specific performance measures in four key areas: financial, customer, internal processes, and learning/growth. It provides a comprehensive view of organizational performance and ensures the strategic plan addresses multiple dimensions of success. Using the PEST analysis, this framework analyzes external factors that could impact the organization, such as Political, Economic, Social, and Technological trends. PEST analysis is particularly useful in industries where external forces shift rapidly, such as technology or healthcare.

An actionable, strategic plan is essential for driving organizational success. By leveraging frameworks like SWOT analysis and SMART goals, leaders can structure their planning process to ensure that it's thorough, realistic, and aligned with the organization's long-term objectives. Regularly revisiting and refining the plan ensures that it remains relevant and flexible in a dynamic environment, ultimately leading to the successful execution of strategic goals.

Chapter 17: Devil's Advocate

Challenging assumptions is essential to critical thinking and effective leadership. Playing devil's advocate is a powerful leadership technique that helps challenge ideas, avoid group thinking, and promote innovation. Leaders can foster a culture of critical thinking and creativity by intentionally questioning assumptions, exploring alternative perspectives, and assessing the validity of decisions.

Effective leaders allow their teams to question the validity and robustness of ideas or solutions. Leaders encourage their teams to think more deeply and critically by challenging prevailing assumptions, leading to refined and well-considered ideas. Leaders who adopt a contrarian position push their team to defend their ideas. This process uncovers potential weaknesses, gaps, or overlooked factors in the team's thinking. A leader should ask tough questions like, "What if this doesn't work?" or "What are the risks we haven't considered?" The final decision or idea becomes stronger and more resilient by forcing the team to think through various scenarios.

Encouraging this method doesn't just expose flaws; it also encourages the team to thoroughly analyze and problem-solve. It pushes people to be better prepared, knowing they must defend their ideas from various angles. For example, during Apple's development of the iPhone, Steve Jobs often played devil's advocate in meetings. He would challenge his team's designs and ideas by taking the opposite stance, forcing them to refine and improve their product until it met his high standards of innovation and user experience.

Leaders should limit group thinking; this occurs when team members prioritize consensus and harmony over critical evaluation. This could lead to poor decision-making and ineffective solutions. Playing devil's advocate disrupts this dynamic by creating an environment where differing opinions and healthy debate are encouraged. This technique prevents teams from falling into the trap of blindly agreeing with the majority or conforming to a dominant viewpoint. When a leader adopts an opposing viewpoint, it permits others to voice alternative perspectives, especially those who may be hesitant to go against the group. This can lead to more diverse opinions and comprehensive discussions, leading to more effective decisions and undiscovered options.

When using this method, creating a safe space for dissent is important. By openly questioning ideas, leaders signal that it's okay to challenge the status quo. This reduces the pressure on team members to conform and encourages them to speak up with their unique viewpoints and ideas. Leaders who actively play devil's advocate can help create a culture where dissent is seen as valuable rather than disruptive. In the 1960s, NASA experienced several instances of groupthink that led to disastrous outcomes, like the Apollo 1 fire. Learning from these mistakes, NASA leaders began incorporating formal devil's advocate sessions in their decision-making processes. This approach helped challenge consensus, allowing engineers to voice previously unspoken concerns, contributing to the success of subsequent missions.

Successful leaders promote innovation; innovation thrives when ideas are challenged and refined through debate. Playing devil's advocate can push teams to think beyond conventional solutions and explore creative alternatives. By questioning assumptions, leaders can help teams break free from limiting beliefs and explore new possibilities by pushing boundaries. When leaders take on the role of devil's advocate, they can challenge the team to think beyond the obvious or the safe option. To challenge your team, you might ask, "What if we did the opposite?" or "Is there a more radical approach we haven't considered?" This forces the team to push the boundaries of their thinking, consider new angles and bolder strategies, and stimulate creativity. This approach prompts people to think more creatively because they are forced to consider alternatives and defend their reasoning. This method encourages divergent thinking, which is critical for innovation. Successful teams explore "what if" scenarios and think creatively to solve complex problems. Netflix's shift from DVD rentals to streaming was born out of questioning the long-term sustainability of its initial business model. By constantly playing devil's advocate and asking questions like, "What if physical DVDs become obsolete?" the leadership team was able to pivot their strategy and lead the streaming revolution, disrupting the entertainment industry. Playing devil's advocate also enhances decision quality by forcing a deeper analysis of potential outcomes, leading to more thoughtful and robust decisions. When leaders challenge their teams to consider worst-case scenarios or alternative outcomes, they better understand the risks and benefits involved in a decision. By forcing the team to think through the downsides of a decision, leaders help them to develop contingency plans or safeguard against risks. The devil's advocate approach helps limit risk mitigation by making the team consider what could go wrong, helping to prevent costly mistakes.

Challenging ideas from different angles ensures a wider range of perspectives is considered. This reduces the chance of blind spots and biases affecting decision-making, leading to more well-rounded and inclusive outcomes. In military leadership, the devil's advocate approach is often used in war gaming and strategic planning. Commanders simulate worst-case scenarios to challenge their teams and ensure they are prepared for a wide range of potential outcomes, improving the quality of their decision-making under pressure.

Fostering a Culture of Continuous Improvement, leaders create an environment where continuous questioning and improvement are the norm. This builds a culture where people don't settle for the first or easiest solution but instead strive for the best one. As a leader, you should always encourage continuous learning and development. Leaders who play devil's advocate emphasize the importance of

109

learning and growth. By questioning ideas, they encourage the team to seek better solutions and not be complacent. This mindset fosters continuous improvement, where individuals and teams always seek ways to evolve and innovate.

Another benefit of this method is that it helps create resiliency. In environments where ideas are constantly challenged, teams become more resilient. They are accustomed to defending their ideas and thinking from all angles, which builds confidence, adaptability, and ownership. Toyota's "Kaizen" philosophy, which emphasizes continuous improvement, involves playing devil's advocate at all levels of the organization. By questioning processes and encouraging employees to find better ways to work, Toyota consistently innovates and improves, becoming a global leader in quality and efficiency.

Devil's advocate is a powerful tool for leaders to challenge ideas, avoid group thinking, and promote innovation. By questioning assumptions, leaders encourage deeper thinking, uncover potential risks, and push their teams toward more creative, robust solutions. This approach fosters an environment where healthy debate, diverse perspectives, and continuous improvement thrive, leading to better decisions and long-term success.

Chapter 18: Hold the Standard

Consistency is key in leadership; maintaining high standards within a team is crucial for delivering consistent, high-quality results, fostering a culture of excellence, and ensuring long-term success. High standards push teams to exceed expectations, innovate, and remain competitive. Holding the team accountable to these standards ensures everyone contributes their best efforts, aligns with organizational goals, and maintains stakeholder trust. However, balancing high standards with a supportive, empowering leadership style is important. Micromanaging can stifle creativity, reduce autonomy, and lead to disengagement. Some strategies to consider maintaining high standards without micromanaging are clear expectations, delegation, ownership, support, feedback, and leading by example.

Be transparent about what success looks like for your team. Define key metrics, deadlines, and quality expectations. When teams understand the "why" behind the standards, they're more motivated to meet them. Regularly revisit these expectations so they stay relevant and at the forefront of their minds. You want to assign tasks

111

to team members based on their strengths and trust them to deliver. Giving autonomy fosters accountability and sets clear outcomes but allows flexibility in achieving them. Avoid over-checking or controlling every step of the process. Encourage problem-solving and initiative. Doing this creates an environment where team members feel responsible for their work. When people have ownership, they're more likely to uphold high standards without constant oversight. Encourage peer accountability within your team; a culture of mutual respect and shared goals naturally drives higher performance.

Avoid over-checking and being controlling; you should still have regular check-ins. This should be seen as an opportunity to provide guidance and resources, not to micromanage. Ask if the team needs help rather than focusing solely on results. Coach them through challenges and help identify solutions, but resist solving problems for them unless necessary. Provide constructive, timely feedback when standards aren't met. Instead of punitive measures, treat it as a learning opportunity to help the team improve. Encourage team members to give feedback on processes and standards. This makes them feel heard and invested in maintaining high quality.

Recognize and reward individuals and teams when they meet or exceed standards. This reinforces positive behavior and motivates others to strive for excellence. Make recognition a regular part of your management so team members are continuously inspired to maintain high performance.

Lead by example, demonstrate the standards you expect through your work ethic and approach. When leaders model excellence, it sets a powerful precedent for the team. By emphasizing clarity, autonomy, and support, leaders can maintain high standards without falling into micromanagement. Trusting the team while offering guidance when needed helps create a motivated, high-performing environment.

Holding the standard requires holding people accountable. Accountability is a vital aspect of a team's performance. Setting clear expectations and consequences for failure is vital to effective leadership and team management. When expectations are communicated, everyone knows what is required of them, and positive and negative consequences are understood in advance. This clarity fosters accountability, helps prevent misunderstandings, and drives consistent performance. However, balancing accountability with a culture that encourages learning, creativity, and risk-taking is equally important. A culture of accountability without fear ensures that people feel responsible for their work without being paralyzed by the potential consequences of failure. Clear expectations align teams around shared goals and ensure everyone works toward the same objectives. Team members may interpret tasks and goals differently without clearly defined expectations, leading to confusion, miscommunication, and underperformance. Setting clear expectations means defining success in measurable, actionable terms without room for ambiguity.

In many tech companies, project managers set clear expectations for product development cycles, including deadlines, deliverables, and quality standards. By providing specific metrics for success, teams can align their efforts, and progress is easily tracked. This clarity reduces confusion and enables faster course correction if things go off track. When expectations are communicated, they provide a basis for fair evaluation. Team members are more likely to view their treatment as equitable when they understand the criteria they are being evaluated against. This consistency builds trust between leaders and their teams, fostering a healthy, cooperative environment. In the military, clear expectations around performance, conduct, and discipline create a culture where fairness and accountability are paramount. Everyone is aware of their duties and responsibilities, and consequences for failure consistently reinforce trust in the system. Clear expectations serve as a roadmap for performance. When employees know what is expected of them, they can better prioritize their tasks, manage their time, and focus their efforts. This leads to improved performance, higher motivation, and greater achievement when goals are met. In organizations like Amazon, performance metrics are highly defined. Employees know precisely what to do to meet targets, which drives them to focus on achieving those goals. This culture of clarity pushes performance and rewards excellence through clearly defined paths for advancement.

Consequences for failure are necessary to reinforce accountability. When team members understand that there are tangible outcomes for failing to meet expectations, they are more likely to take their responsibilities seriously. However, consequences should be proportional and tied to the severity of the failure. Not all failures should result in punishment; many can be learning opportunities. In sports, consequences for failing to meet performance goals might include losing a starting position or being benched. These consequences are clearly understood in advance, so when enforced, they reinforce the idea that performance matters. However, many coaches also use these moments to work on weaknesses and help the athlete improve.

Consequences for meeting or exceeding expectations are just as important as failing. Recognizing and rewarding success helps reinforce the behaviors and efforts you want to see. Positive reinforcement encourages a culture where people strive to meet and exceed expectations. Companies like Salesforce and Google have recognition programs that celebrate team members who meet or exceed expectations. These rewards come in the form of bonuses, promotions, and public recognition, all of which create a culture where people are motivated to perform at their best because success is celebrated.

Not all failures warrant punishment; some failures are necessary for growth and innovation. When leaders set clear expectations but create room for failure as a learning opportunity, they build a culture where teams feel safe to take risks. The consequence of failure in such cases should be to reflect, learn, and improve. At Pixar, failure is considered a critical part of the creative process. The studio encourages its teams to try new ideas, knowing that not all will succeed. When failures happen, they're treated as learning moments, with leaders facilitating discussions on what went wrong and how it can be improved. This culture of "failing forward" allows Pixar to consistently innovate without a paralyzing fear of failure. It's important to communicate that while there are consequences for underperformance or failure, these consequences are fair and tied to improvement. The goal should be to encourage learning and growth rather than instill fear. When consequences are tied to development rather than punishment, it creates a culture where accountability is embraced without anxiety. Netflix is known for its high-performance culture, where employees are expected to meet high standards. While accountability is strong, the company also emphasizes that employees should take ownership of mistakes and learn from them. There is no culture of fear if someone fails; they are expected to reflect and improve. However, if someone repeatedly fails to meet expectations, the company moves quickly to make changes, maintaining accountability fairly and transparently.

Leaders should model the behavior they expect from their teams. If a leader is willing to admit their own mistakes and take accountability, it creates a culture where employees feel safe doing the same. Leaders who avoid blame-shifting and show how they learn from their failures set a powerful example for their teams. In 2020, when New Zealand Prime Minister Jacinda Ardern admitted her government made mistakes in handling aspects of the COVID-

19 response, she did so openly and transparently. This honesty reinforced trust with her people.

In leadership, holding the standard is essential because it establishes a foundation of trust, respect, and integrity. When leaders consistently uphold high standards, they set a clear example for others to follow, fostering an environment of accountability and excellence. This commitment inspires those around them to meet, and often exceed expectations, creating a cohesive team that strives toward common goals with dedication and purpose. Ultimately, maintaining standards isn't just about personal integrity; it's about shaping a culture where everyone is motivated to perform at their best, making the entire organization stronger and more resilient.

Chapter 19: Recognition

Recognizing effort motivates people; it is important to recognize both big and small achievements. Leaders should always look for different ways to reward team members, from public acknowledgment to career advancement. Recognizing big and small achievements help foster a positive and motivated workplace. Employees' feeling valued and appreciated enhances their engagement, satisfaction, and overall productivity. Recognition also helps reinforce the behaviors that contribute to team and organizational success while boosting morale and creating a culture of appreciation. Recognizing individual and team accomplishments motivates employees to continue performing at a high level. Even small wins, when acknowledged, create a sense of pride and purpose. Employees are more likely to be engaged when they know their efforts are valued. When an organization regularly recognizes achievements, it cultivates a positive and inclusive culture. Recognition promotes mutual respect and teamwork, leading to better collaboration and increased morale.

Publicly acknowledging big achievements and small daily efforts encourages others to emulate those behaviors. Recognizing positive contributions, such as meeting goals, innovation, or displaying leadership, sets a standard for excellence. This can also help increase retention and reduce turnover; employees who feel valued and recognized for their contributions are likelier to stay with the company. Recognition programs help create a sense of loyalty and belonging, reducing the likelihood of turnover. When employees are recognized for their contributions, it can also lead to opportunities for growth, such as promotions, new responsibilities, or professional development. This contributes to long-term career satisfaction and builds a pathway for career advancement. Research shows that employees who are regularly recognized are more productive and committed. Recognition increases engagement, enhancing individual and team performance and improving business outcomes.

There are many ways to reward and recognize your team. It can take many forms, and it's important to tailor it to the needs and preferences of the recognized individuals. Here is where knowing what motivates your people is important. It can range from simply offering words of appreciation in meetings or conversations that can make a big impact. For example, publicly thanking a team member for their hard work in a project meeting helps reinforce their efforts in front of peers. Highlighting accomplishments in a companywide email, newsletter, or team meeting provides recognition beyond immediate colleagues. It allows employees to be acknowledged by leadership and peers across the organization.

There are also more formal programs that recognize outstanding performance over time, offer public acknowledgment, and motivate others to strive for excellence. Monetary recognition, such as bonuses, spot awards, or gift cards, is a way to reward high performance. It shows that the company values the employee's efforts and is willing to invest in their satisfaction. In some organizations, you can also give a personalized gift. A thoughtful, personalized gift based on an employee's interests can show a level of care that goes beyond generic rewards. For instance, a team member who loves books might appreciate a gift card to their favorite bookstore.

Promoting employees who consistently demonstrate strong performance clearly acknowledges their skills and contributions. It also serves as motivation for others to strive for similar advancement. Assigning high performers to leadership roles in projects or teams allows them to grow and be recognized for their ability to take on responsibility. These can increase professional development. Sponsoring employee training programs, certifications, or conferences is also a valuable way to recognize their potential and invest in their long-term growth.

Along with individual rewards, you can also have team celebrations. Organizing team lunches, dinners, or offsite events to celebrate the completion of a project or hitting a major milestone is a way to recognize the team's collective effort. You can also recognize work anniversaries or tenure if there are no noteworthy accomplishments during that period. Acknowledging work anniversaries or tenure milestones demonstrates that the organization values long-term commitment. This can include certificates, awards, or even sabbaticals for long-term employees.

Rewarding employees with additional paid time off or an extra vacation day for their hard work can be an appreciated form of recognition. It shows that the organization cares about the employees' work-life balance. Offering flexible schedules or remote work options as a reward for outstanding performance demonstrates trust in the employee's autonomy and is a nonmonetary way of recognizing achievement.

All of these are fairly simple for a leader to accomplish, but some of the harder approaches based on policy could be more external recognition. Nominating employees for industry awards or other forms of external recognition, rewards the individual and boosts the organization's reputation as a place that fosters excellence. Establishing a formalized recognition program, such as peer-nominated or leadership-selected awards, can be made easier by providing structured ways to acknowledge achievements consistently.

One of the most underrated forms of recognition is a personal letter from leadership. A personalized letter or email from a senior leader acknowledging an employee's contribution can have significant impact. Knowing that their work is recognized by top leadership builds confidence and loyalty. Following up with all of these should lead to an individual development plan. Engaging in one-on-one discussions about career aspirations and offering pathways for growth is another way to recognize an employee's contributions. Providing mentorship or coaching can be both a reward and an investment in their future success.

Recognizing big and small achievements is crucial in motivating teams, promoting a positive culture, and reinforcing desired behaviors. Recognition can take many forms, from public acknowledgment to personalized rewards, career advancement, and flexible work arrangements. Tailoring recognition to individual preferences and making it a regular part of the company's culture ensures that employees feel valued, appreciated, and motivated to contribute to the team's success. By fostering a culture of recognition, organizations can improve employee engagement, satisfaction, and retention while driving overall performance.

Chapter 20: No Excuses

Action beats hesitation, and encouraging leaders to focus on solutions rather than excuses is crucial for fostering resilience, adaptability, and progress. Leaders who embrace this mindset take responsibility, inspire their teams, and navigate challenges with an action-oriented approach. By focusing on solutions, leaders create an environment where innovation flourishes, accountability is central to growth, while excuses erode trust and slow momentum. Bold actions, especially in uncertain times, demonstrate leadership and inspire others to follow suit.

Leaders who focus on solutions demonstrate accountability. By owning up to problems rather than shifting blame, they build trust with their teams, peers, and stakeholders. This trust is vital for maintaining morale and fostering a culture where challenges are viewed as opportunities for growth rather than setbacks. Solutions-oriented leadership boosts the confidence of those around them. When a leader is proactive, they communicate that they are in control, even in uncertainty. This instills a sense of stability and direction within the team, reducing anxiety and improving performance. When leaders adopt a no-excuses mentality, they create an environment where people feel encouraged to think creatively and solve problems. The focus shifts from what went wrong to how it can be fixed, fostering innovation and encouraging people to push beyond limitations. Leaders are role models; focusing on solutions sets the tone for how their teams approach problems. They demonstrate that setbacks are part of the process but should never define the outcome. This mentality promotes perseverance and resilience across the organization.

Winston Churchill's leadership during World War II exemplifies focusing on solutions in the face of overwhelming uncertainty. When Britain stood alone against the Nazi regime after the fall of France, Churchill refused to make excuses or surrender to fear. His famous "We shall never surrender" speech galvanized a nation on the brink of collapse. Despite the enormous threat, Churchill's bold decision to resist Hitler was a turning point in the war. His resolve and focus on solutions, such as fostering alliances with the U.S. and the Soviet Union, proved pivotal in the Allied victory. Elon Musk faced tremendous uncertainty when trying to make SpaceX a viable company. The company had several rocket failures between 2006 and 2008, jeopardizing the entire project. Musk could have blamed technology, external conditions, or even the financial crisis, but instead, he pushed ahead. After multiple failures, SpaceX successfully launched the Falcon 1 in 2008. Musk's solution-oriented focus has since revolutionized space travel, pushing boundaries many believed were impossible. Faced with the economic devastation of the Great Depression, Franklin D. Roosevelt didn't dwell on the economy's collapse or make excuses for previous administrations. Instead, he focused on bold, solution-driven initiatives through the New Deal. Despite fierce opposition, he implemented wide-reaching reforms and programs like social security, unemployment insurance, and infrastructure projects that helped stabilize the country. His willingness to act in the face of uncertainty was critical in restoring hope and reviving the American economy. They all made tough decisions quickly, even without all the information, because they understand that waiting for certainty often leads to missed opportunities.

Leaders must also have adaptability, visionary thinking, and resilience. Solution-focused leaders know that plans may need to evolve and are willing to pivot when necessary. Instead of getting bogged down in the problem, they focus on long-term solutions to create lasting change. They persevere in the face of adversity, learning from failures rather than allowing them to become excuses for inaction. Encouraging leaders to focus on solutions rather than excuses helps cultivate a culture of accountability, innovation, and progress. Leaders who act boldly, despite uncertainty, inspire confidence and drive positive change. Whether in moments of crisis or day-to-day challenges, the ability to embrace solutions and take decisive action defines effective leadership. Leaders like Churchill, Musk, and Roosevelt prove that it's not the absence of challenges but how one responds to them that ultimately defines success.

Chapter 21: Attainable Goals Extraordinary Expectations

Goals should be realistic, but expectations should inspire growth. Striking a balance between pushing for excellence and setting achievable goals is a hallmark of effective leadership. The key is challenging teams to grow and perform at their highest potential without overwhelming them or creating unattainable expectations. Leaders who master this balance foster high performance, motivation, and resilience while maintaining a healthy work culture.

Stretched goals push employees beyond their comfort zones, encouraging innovation and growth. However, they should remain realistic and within reach. Stretch goals are challenging but achievable with effort, and they should be broken down into smaller, manageable milestones. Jeff Bezos of Amazon often pushed his team with bold, innovative goals, like expanding Amazon from an online bookstore to an "everything store." However, these ambitious objectives were supported by clear, achievable steps. He balanced audacity with incremental growth, fostering a culture that sought excellence without setting teams up for failure.

126

Leaders who cultivate a growth mindset in their teams emphasize that challenges and setbacks are learning opportunities. This mindset encourages employees to take on difficult tasks without fear of failure, knowing that growth comes from effort and perseverance. Satya Nadella, CEO of Microsoft, transformed the company's culture by promoting a growth mindset. Rather than focusing on perfection, Nadella encouraged employees to learn from mistakes and continuously improve. This shift helped Microsoft pursue bold initiatives, such as expanding into cloud computing while keeping employees motivated and resilient.

When pushing for excellence, it's important to clearly define success and provide the necessary resources, training, and support to help the team achieve those goals. Setting clear expectations helps employees understand what is required and avoids confusion about the desired outcomes. Former PepsiCo CEO Indra Nooyi was known for her high expectations and ensuring her teams had the resources and support they needed to succeed. She encouraged her employees to take risks and innovate, particularly in expanding their product line to include healthier options. Still, she provided clear direction and access to tools that ensured they could meet these ambitious goals.

Excellence is often achieved through teamwork. Leaders can set ambitious goals encouraging collaboration, where team members support one another in achieving a common objective. Shared accountability ensures that individuals don't feel solely responsible for daunting tasks and fosters a collaborative effort toward excellence. Elon Musk challenges his teams at Tesla and SpaceX with ambitious goals like building electric cars at scale or sending humans to Mars. While these objectives are extraordinarily difficult, Musk emphasizes collaboration and shared accountability. Teams are encouraged to work together to solve problems, and the company is known for a culture that values individual contribution and collective effort.

Leaders must offer timely and constructive feedback to keep employees on track toward excellence without setting them up for failure. Recognize progress and accomplishments, even if the goal hasn't been achieved. Celebrating small wins builds momentum and keeps teams motivated for the larger challenge. Mary Barra, CEO of General Motors, fosters a culture of accountability and continuous improvement. She sets high expectations for her teams, provides regular feedback, and acknowledges progress, especially in GM's transformation toward electric vehicles. This helps keep teams motivated without feeling overwhelmed by the scale of the challenge.

Excellence doesn't always come from rigidly sticking to a plan. Allowing flexibility in how teams achieve their goals gives them the autonomy to be creative and find solutions that work best for them. Flexibility fosters innovation and helps employees feel empowered rather than constrained. Under former CEO Eric Schmidt, Google's leadership implemented the OKR (Objectives and Key Results) framework, encouraging teams to set ambitious goals. However, the framework also allowed flexibility in how teams approached these goals, promoting creativity and ownership over the processes while striving for excellence.

Set goals that align with the strengths and capabilities of the team. While challenging employees is important, the goals should remain within their expertise and skills. This ensures that the challenges stretch their abilities but remain achievable. Steve Jobs was known for pushing his teams to deliver excellence, particularly in product design and user experience. While Jobs set high standards, he also recognized the unique talents within his team and aligned their tasks with their strengths. This approach allowed for ambitious goals, like the creation of the iPhone, without overwhelming his team.

Leaders who push for excellence must be adaptive and recognize when goals must be adjusted based on changing circumstances. If a team struggles due to unforeseen obstacles, leaders should reassess the goals and provide new strategies or resources to ensure success. This prevents burnout and frustration, ensuring the team remains motivated and can achieve excellence. Alan Mulally, the former CEO of Ford, demonstrated this balance during the financial crisis when he pushed the company toward excellence by restructuring its operations. However, he was also flexible in his approach, making adjustments based on the realities of the situation while continuing to challenge his teams to think long-term.

Effective leaders know how to set ambitious goals that are just within reach. For example, challenging a team to increase revenue by 20% may be difficult but achievable with the right strategies.

However, setting a goal of 100% growth may be unrealistic and demotivating. The key is to stretch the team without creating the perception that the goal is impossible. Leaders can encourage excellence without fear of failure by creating a culture where it's safe to take risks and learn from mistakes. This encourages employees to innovate and strive for excellence without the anxiety of perfectionism. Failure is seen as a step toward improvement rather than a personal or professional setback.

Micromanaging can stifle creativity and prevent employees from reaching their full potential Great leaders set high expectations but give their teams the freedom to determine the best way to meet those expectations. This autonomy allows employees to take ownership of their work, resulting in higher levels of engagement and a stronger drive for excellence. Leaders who push for excellence also ensure that their teams feel psychologically safe to express concerns or admit when they're struggling. Creating an open environment where employees can discuss challenges without fear of retribution prevents burnout and allows for timely intervention when adjustments are needed.

Leaders can balance pushing for excellence while setting achievable goals by setting stretch objectives, fostering a growth mindset, and ensuring the necessary support and resources are available. Leaders can challenge their teams by providing clarity, recognizing progress, promoting collaboration, and being flexible without setting them up for failure. Historical examples of leaders like Bezos, Nadella, and Jobs highlight the importance of balancing high expectations with achievable, incremental steps, driving their teams to greatness without compromising their well-being or success.

Chapter 22: What Got You Here Won't Get You There

You can have change without progress, but you can't have progress without change! Constant growth and evolution are a necessity for improvement. Continuous learning and adaptation are critical to effective leadership, particularly in today's rapidly changing world. Leaders who remain static or rely solely on past successes risk falling behind. At the same time, those who commit to lifelong learning and evolving their skills are better equipped to navigate new challenges, inspire their teams, and drive innovation. Adapting and growing is no longer optional but essential for leadership success. Leaders must continually update their knowledge and skills to stay relevant in an era of technological advancements, globalization, and shifting market dynamics. What worked yesterday may not work tomorrow, and leaders unwilling to evolve may struggle to guide their organizations through change. Bill Gates, the co-founder of Microsoft, is a leader known for his commitment to continuous learning. Even after stepping down from Microsoft, Gates has remained an avid reader and learner, constantly adapting his knowledge base to address global challenges like public health and climate change. His ability to evolve with the times has kept him influential long after his tenure as CEO.

Disruptions in the form of new competitors, economic shifts, or unexpected crises (such as the COVID-19 pandemic) require leaders to adapt quickly and make decisions in unfamiliar contexts. Continuous learning helps leaders stay agile and prepared to pivot their strategies in response to these disruptions. Satya Nadella exemplifies adaptive leadership. When he took over, as CEO of Microsoft, it was seen as lagging in cloud computing. Nadella's focus on continuous learning and openness to new ideas enabled him to successfully shift Microsoft's focus to cloud-based solutions, a major factor in the company's resurgence.

Today's leaders manage increasingly diverse teams spanning different generations, cultures, and geographies. Continuous learning helps leaders better understand the unique needs of their workforce and adapt their leadership style to foster inclusion, collaboration, and productivity. Indra Nooyi, former CEO of PepsiCo, constantly sought to understand different cultural perspectives and generational trends to better connect with employees and customers. Her adaptability allowed her to lead the company in diversifying its product line and responding to shifts in consumer demand, all while fostering a people-centered leadership style.

Innovation often comes from a willingness to learn and explore new ideas. Leaders prioritizing continuous learning foster a culture of curiosity and experimentation within their organizations, driving creativity and encouraging employees to think outside the box. Jeff Bezos, the founder of Amazon, encouraged a "Day 1 thinking culture," emphasizing a startup mentality and constant learning, even as Amazon grew into a giant corporation. His leadership focus on innovation and continuous adaptation helped Amazon disrupt numerous industries.

Emotional intelligence is a vital skill for leaders, and continuous learning helps leaders strengthen their self-awareness, empathy, and ability to manage relationships. As teams evolve and the workplace becomes more complex, leaders must adapt their communication and interpersonal skills to maintain trust and inspire their people. Former CEO of Ford, Alan Mulally, led with emotional intelligence and was known for creating a culture of trust and transparency. His ability to adapt his leadership style and build strong relationships with employees allowed him to successfully guide Ford through a difficult financial period.

The unpredictable nature of the modern business environment requires leaders to be comfortable with ambiguity. Continuous learning fosters an adaptable mindset, enabling leaders to confidently approach uncertainty and devise innovative solutions for emerging challenges. During the global financial crisis, Howard Schultz returned to Starbucks as CEO. His commitment to learning and ability to adapt quickly allowed him to refocus the company's priorities, closed underperforming stores, and navigate the business through a turbulent time, ultimately revitalizing the brand.

Leaders must adopt a growth mindset, believing skills and intelligence can be developed through effort, learning, and experience. This mindset encourages leaders to embrace challenges, persist through setbacks, and see failure as an opportunity for growth. Leaders can evolve by continually seeking feedback, taking on new challenges, and investing time in self-development. They should also encourage their teams to adopt this mindset, fostering a culture where learning is valued.

With rapid technological advancements, leaders must stay informed about artificial intelligence, automation, and data analytics trends. Leaders don't need to be experts in every technology, but they must understand how these tools can impact their industry and how to leverage them for success. Leaders can attend workshops, take online courses, or seek expert mentorship in areas where they need to improve their understanding. Being open to new technologies and understanding their potential will enable leaders to guide their organizations through digital transformations. Leadership styles must evolve based on the changing needs of the workforce and the external environment. For example, the shift to remote work has required leaders to be more empathetic, communicative, and flexible in managing teams. Leaders who adapt their style to fit these new demands will be more successful. Leaders should assess their leadership style and identify areas where adaptation is necessary. An example would be if they tend to be hands-on; they may need to learn to delegate more and trust their teams to work independently, especially in remote or hybrid work settings. Leaders must continually broaden their horizons by exposing themselves to diverse perspectives. Whether through reading, networking, or engaging with different cultures, expanding one's worldview allows leaders to be more inclusive and responsive to various challenges. Leaders can participate in diverse networks, attend industry conferences, or seek mentorship from individuals from different backgrounds. This enriches their perspective and helps them adapt to the needs of a global and diverse workforce.

Modern leaders must also adapt by prioritizing their well-being and that of their teams. Burnout and stress are increasingly prevalent, and leaders must evolve their approach to ensure a balance between achieving organizational goals and maintaining a healthy, supportive work environment. Leaders should adopt practices that promote mental and physical health, such as flexible working arrangements and employee well-being programs. By modeling a balanced approach to work, leaders can inspire their teams to maintain productivity without sacrificing personal health. Leadership is not a destination but a journey that requires a lifelong commitment to learning. Leaders must continually seek new knowledge, develop new skills, and stay informed about industry trends. Leaders can set personal development goals, regularly attend workshops or seminars, and make time for reading or formal education. Learning should be an ongoing priority, not something that happens sporadically.

Continuous learning and adaptation are indispensable for modern leaders who want to succeed in a dynamic and ever-changing world.

Whether it's keeping pace with new technologies, responding to disruptions, or fostering a culture of innovation, leaders must commit to lifelong learning and evolving their leadership styles to meet new challenges. Leaders like Nadella, Nooyi, and Schultz have demonstrated the power of adaptability and continuous growth, proving that those who stay curious and open to change are the ones who lead their teams and organizations to lasting success.

Chapter 23: Success Is in the Work You're Avoiding

Avoidance often hides opportunities; tackling uncomfortable tasks, those we naturally avoid due to fear, difficulty, or uncertainty, is one of the most direct paths to personal and professional growth. In leadership, the work we resist doing often holds the key to success because it forces us to confront our limitations, expand our capabilities, and gain new insights. While avoiding difficult tasks may make us feel more comfortable in the short term, it can hinder our progress and limit our potential. Addressing uncomfortable work or situations head-on is a trait shared by many successful leaders. These leaders often find discomfort leads to breakthroughs, innovation, and lasting growth. When leaders engage with challenging tasks, whether having tough conversations, learning new skills, or confronting failure, they step outside their comfort zones. This discomfort creates space for growth, as it pushes leaders to develop resilience, adaptability, and new competencies. Tackling uncomfortable tasks is key to growth and expands capabilities. Taking on difficult tasks allows leaders to build new skills, gain confidence, and enhance their ability to handle complexity. These tasks often require creative problem-solving, deeper thinking, and sustained focus, all contributing to personal development.

Discomfort and challenges are inevitable in leadership, and the more often leaders face them, the stronger their resilience becomes. Leaders who tackle uncomfortable work head-on learn how to bounce back from setbacks and remain persistent in adversity. Innovation often occurs when leaders are forced to solve difficult problems. By confronting challenges, leaders open themselves to new ideas, approaches, and perspectives they might not have considered otherwise. The difficult tasks we avoid often reveal our insecurities, weaknesses, or fears. By confronting these tasks, leaders gain greater self-awareness and clarity about their values, limitations, and goals. Several well-known leaders have found success by embracing the hard, uncomfortable tasks others shy away from. Their stories demonstrate how stepping into discomfort not only leads to personal growth but also paves the way for innovation and organizational success.

Steve Jobs is often celebrated as a visionary leader, but his journey to success was riddled with discomfort and failure. In 1985, Jobs was ousted from the company he co-founded, Apple. This was an incredibly painful and uncomfortable moment for him, but instead of giving up, Jobs tackled the challenge of starting over. Jobs founded NeXT, a new computer company, and acquired Pixar, where he was forced to tackle unfamiliar and uncomfortable challenges in the animation industry. His discomfort with being outside his original industry forced him to innovate, leading Pixar to produce Toy Story, the first-ever feature-length computer-animated film. Eventually, Apple acquired NeXT, bringing Jobs back to the company and positioning him to lead the revolution that produced the iPhone, iPod, and iPad. Jobs' willingness to face discomfort, reinvent himself, and learning from failure played a major role in his growth as a leader and Apple's success.

Sara Blakely, founder of Spanx, is another leader who embraced uncomfortable tasks to achieve her success. Early in her career, Blakely worked as a Dorsoduro fax machine salesperson. She faced rejection daily during this time but pushed through it, using these experiences to build resilience and learn how to sell her ideas. When she came up with the idea for Spanx, Blakely encountered several uncomfortable challenges. She had no fashion industry experience, business background, and limited resources. Undeterred, she tackled these obstacles head-on. She cold-called manufacturers, faced skepticism from industry insiders, and personally handled everything from patent applications to distribution. Blakely built Spanx into a billion-dollar company through persistence and willingness to do what others avoided. Blakely's success is a testament to how tackling uncomfortable tasks like constant rejection and navigating unfamiliar territory can lead to incredible breakthroughs.

Walt Disney, one of the most iconic figures in entertainment history, faced enormous discomfort and failure throughout his career. Early on, Disney's first film company went bankrupt, and he was told by others in the industry that his ideas wouldn't work. He was also frequently short on funds and struggled to keep his creative visions afloat. Despite these challenges, Disney confronted the risks and uncertainties head-on. His decision to create the world's first feature-length animated film, Snow White and the Seven Dwarfs, was considered a massive gamble, with many experts predicting it would fail. Disney had to overcome financial difficulties, technical limitations, and skepticism from his team. The discomfort he faced in bringing his vision to life paid off when Snow White became a groundbreaking success, laying the foundation for the Disney empire. Disney's story illustrates that confronting uncertainty and taking bold risks, especially when uncomfortable, is often the path to long-term success.

Leaders looking to grow must make a habit of facing uncomfortable tasks rather than avoiding them. If tackling a big, uncomfortable task seems overwhelming, start small. Break the task into manageable pieces and gradually work your way up. As you gain confidence by completing smaller challenges, you'll build the momentum needed to take on larger, more complex ones. Change the way you perceive discomfort. Instead of viewing it as something to be avoided, reframe it as an opportunity for growth. Recognize that pushing through discomfort helps you learn, develop resilience, and build new skills. Hold yourself accountable for facing difficult tasks, even when you don't feel like it. Set clear deadlines, share your goals with a trusted colleague or mentor, and track your progress to ensure you're taking action. One of the primary reasons we avoid uncomfortable tasks is the fear of failure. Rather than avoiding failure, embrace it as part of the learning process. Recognize that failure provides valuable lessons and is a necessary steppingstone to success. Surround yourself with people who encourage growth and hold you accountable. Whether it's a mentor, coach, or supportive colleague, having a network of people who challenge you to face difficult tasks will increase your resilience and motivation.

Leaders who consistently tackle uncomfortable tasks see significant personal and professional growth in the long run. By doing the hard work that others avoid, these leaders develop the skills, resilience, and adaptability necessary for long-term success. Leaders who regularly confront difficult tasks become more confident decision-makers. They learn to handle complexity, weigh risks, and make bold choices that drive innovation. Leaders who model the ability to tackle uncomfortable work inspire their teams to do the same. By embracing challenges, they create a culture of resilience, persistence, and growth within their organizations. Leaders who are not afraid to face the uncomfortable work others avoid are more likely to innovate, grow, and lead their organizations to new heights. They see obstacles as opportunities where others hesitate and position themselves for greater success and personal growth. Whether confronting failure, learning new skills, or addressing difficult situations, the discomfort these tasks bring helps leaders develop resilience, expand their capabilities, and achieve long-term success. Leaders like Jobs, Blakely, and Disney exemplify how facing difficult work head-on can lead to extraordinary achievements. By embracing discomfort and pushing through challenges, leaders unlock their full potential and inspire others to do the same.

Chapter 24: Unfaced Fears Become Limits

Fear limits leadership potential and embracing discomfort can help lead to growth. Fear can be one of the most significant barriers to effective leadership. It manifests in various ways, such as fear of failure, rejection, conflict, or even success, and can lead to indecision, hesitation, and a reluctance to take bold actions. Leaders who let fear dictate their decisions limit their growth and the potential of their team or organization. However, when leaders embrace discomfort and confront their fears, they unlock their potential and open the door to innovation, growth, and lasting success. Fear creates mental and emotional blocks that hinder leadership in various ways. It can distort decision-making, inhibit creativity, and prevent leaders from taking necessary risks.

Many leaders fear making mistakes, leading to inaction or overly cautious decision-making. Avoiding failure often stifles innovation and prevents leaders from taking the risks needed to achieve great outcomes. Some leaders avoid difficult conversations or decisions because they fear creating tension or conflict. This can result in unresolved issues, a lack of accountability, and a weakened team culture.

The fear of being judged or rejected by peers, employees, or stakeholders can make leaders hesitant to voice their true opinions, propose bold ideas, or make unpopular decisions. Surprisingly, some leaders fear the responsibility and pressure that come with success. This fear can cause them to self-sabotage or hold back from pursuing ambitious goals. Leaders who fear making mistakes often overanalyze situations and struggle to make timely decisions. This indecision can create a stagnant work environment and slow progress. Leaders who fear rejection may avoid sharing their true thoughts or take on personas that aren't authentic, which erodes trust with their teams. Fear of failure discourages leaders from encouraging experimentation or risk-taking, leading to a risk-averse culture that avoids bold ideas and innovation. When fear governs a leader's decision, it weakens their confidence and diminishes their influence. This lack of confidence can trickle down to the team, reducing morale and productivity. Growth begins when leaders are willing to face their fears and step into uncomfortable situations. Embracing discomfort forces leaders to stretch beyond their comfort zones, learn from mistakes, and adapt to new challenges. The discomfort accompanying risk and uncertainty is necessary for personal and organizational growth.

Taking on challenging and uncomfortable tasks broadens a leader's skill set, making them more adaptable and resilient in the face of adversity. When leaders allow themselves and their teams to

145

take risks, they create a culture of experimentation that fosters creativity and innovation. Even if an idea fails, trying something new can generate valuable insights. Each time leaders confront a fear or discomfort, they build confidence in their ability to handle future challenges. This resilience enables them to navigate tough situations more effectively in the future. Leaders who face their fears develop a deeper understanding of themselves and are more likely to lead authentically. Authentic leadership builds trust and respect within teams, encouraging open communication and collaboration.

Abraham Lincoln is often celebrated as one of America's greatest presidents, but his path to success was fraught with repeated failures and setbacks. Before becoming president, Lincoln faced numerous personal and professional defeats: he lost several elections, experienced business failures, and struggled with periods of depression. Despite these challenges, Lincoln persevered. One of Lincoln's most significant moments of fear came during the American Civil War when the fate of the Union hung in the balance. Many doubted his leadership, and Lincoln faced overwhelming pressure to seek peace with the Confederacy. Rather than letting fear dictate his actions, Lincoln embraced the discomfort of leading a divided nation. He made difficult decisions, such as the Emancipation Proclamation, and refused to compromise on his vision of a unified country. Lincoln's ability to face his fears and lead with conviction during one of the most turbulent periods in American history solidified his legacy as a transformative leader.

Oprah Winfrey is a modern example of a leader who has faced her fears head-on. Born into poverty and overcoming a traumatic childhood, Winfrey could have easily been held back by fear, fear of rejection, failure, and vulnerability. Early in her career, as she transitioned from news anchor to talk show host, she faced criticism for being "too emotional" and vulnerable on screen. Instead of shying away from her authentic self, Winfrey embraced her vulnerability and turned it into her greatest strength. She openly shared her struggles and traumas with her audience, creating a deep emotional connection with millions of viewers. Her willingness to be vulnerable helped her rise to fame and paved the way for a new style of talk show centered on empathy, personal growth, and real connection. Winfrey's success demonstrates how facing the discomfort of vulnerability can lead to authenticity and lasting influence.

Howard Schultz faced significant fears when he led Starbucks through a period of rapid global expansion. Schultz envisioned turning Starbucks into a global brand, but he feared that expanding too quickly would dilute the company's core values and unique customer experience. When Starbucks began to falter in the mid-2000s due to overexpansion and a loss of focus, Schultz made the uncomfortable decision to close underperforming stores and refocus on the company's foundational values. He brought the company back to its roots by prioritizing quality, customer experience, and innovation despite the discomfort of reversing years of expansion. Schultz's ability to face the fear of failure and make tough, unpopular decisions helped Starbucks regain profitability and strengthen its brand globally.

The first step in overcoming fear is acknowledging it. Reflect on the areas of leadership that make you uncomfortable, whether it's public speaking, making tough decisions, or confronting team members. Understanding your fears allows you to take steps to address and overcome them. Start by facing smaller fears and building your way up. For example, if you fear confrontation, address minor conflicts with individuals before tackling larger team issues. Each time you step out of your comfort zone, you'll build confidence in handling discomfort. Reframe discomfort and fear as opportunities for growth. Instead of seeing fear as a sign of weakness, view it as a natural part of leadership and a chance to learn. By approaching challenges with a growth mindset, you'll be more willing to take risks and embrace uncertainty. By surrounding yourself with support, it creates a safety net that comforts you in the idea of failure. Seek mentors, coaches, or colleagues who can provide guidance and encouragement as you confront your fears. A support system helps you stay accountable and provides reassurance during tough times. Reflect on what you've learned when you face discomfort or fear and come out the other side. Use failures as learning experiences and celebrate successes as evidence of your ability to grow and evolve as a leader. Understand that fear limits leadership potential by creating barriers to decision-making, stifling innovation, and preventing leaders from taking the bold actions necessary for growth. However, leaders unlock their potential for success by embracing discomfort and confronting fears. Leaders like Lincoln, Winfrey, and Schultz are examples of how facing fears and making tough decisions can lead to greatness. Leaders grow personally and inspire their teams to reach new heights by regularly challenging their fears. Embracing discomfort is the key to unlocking growth, innovation, and authentic leadership.

Chapter 25: The Spotlight

Leaders should remain mindful of how both employees and the public perceive them. Public perception plays a pivotal role in leadership, often shaping how leaders are remembered and the impact of their decisions. It can make or break a leader's legacy, influencing trust, credibility, and authority. Leaders who handle public perception well can harness it to rally support, while those who struggle with it can see their leadership unravel, regardless of their competence or intentions.

Many great leaders endured and handled public perception in a positive manner. Nelson Mandela is often cited as a leader who masterfully managed public perception. His approach to leadership centered around reconciliation, humility, and his unwavering commitment to justice earned him global admiration. Despite spending 27 years in prison, Mandela emerged as a symbol of forgiveness and unity in South Africa. His ability to maintain dignity and foster hope despite intense personal hardship shaped the public's perception of him as a leader of integrity and vision. Another would be Angela Merkel, former Chancellor of Germany, known for her pragmatic and steady leadership. Merkel projected an image of calm competence and careful decision-making, especially during the European financial crisis and the migrant crisis. Her style of understated, facts-based communication built trust over her 16-year tenure. Merkel's ability to rise above partisan politics and lead with a sense of duty to her country made her one of the most respected leaders globally. As the first African American president of the United States, Barack Obama understood the importance of public perception. His eloquent communication, use of digital platforms, and charisma helped shape his image as a progressive and hopeful leader. He navigated polarizing issues with a focus on empathy and inclusion, successfully leveraging public opinion to push forward significant policies. Obama's emphasis on optimism and forward-looking rhetoric resonated deeply with national and international audiences.

Then, some leaders have struggled with public perception. Richard Nixon's presidency is a prime example of how negative public perception can bring down a leader. Although he achieved major diplomatic successes, such as opening relations with China and the détente with the Soviet Union, the Watergate scandal damaged his reputation. His secretive behavior, attempts to cover up illegal actions, and eventual resignation left him as a symbol of dishonesty and abuse of power. Nixon's inability to manage the fallout from Watergate highlighted how public mistrust can destroy even the most powerful leaders. Theresa May, the former U.K. Prime Minister, struggled significantly with public perception during her leadership of the Brexit negotiations. Her public image was often seen as rigid and disconnected, which hindered her ability to unite a divided government and country. The perception that she could not deliver a clear and decisive Brexit deal led to her resignation. Despite her efforts, her leadership was overshadowed by a lack of communication and strategic adaptability in the eyes of the public and her peers. Another is Elizabeth Holmes, founder of Theranos. Elizabeth Holmes initially positioned herself as a visionary leader in healthcare technology. Her charismatic public appearances and media-savvy style helped Theranos gain significant investment and attention. However, when it was revealed that her company's technology was fraudulent, Holmes' public image collapsed. Her fall from grace illustrates how public perception, especially in an era of intense media scrutiny, can rapidly shift when leaders are perceived as dishonest or misleading.

Leaders who effectively manage public perception often excel in transparency, communication, and empathy. They understand that while they cannot control every aspect of public opinion, they can shape their narrative by being authentic and maintaining clear, consistent communication. Leaders like Jacinda Ardern of New Zealand have gained international recognition for leading authentically and empathically, particularly during crises like the Christchurch Mosque attacks and the COVID-19 pandemic. Leaders who are upfront about challenges and failures tend to maintain public trust even during difficult times. Franklin D. Roosevelt's "Fireside Chats" during the Great Depression are a famous example of how direct, transparent communication can build public confidence.

Public perception is a double-edged sword in leadership. Leaders who cultivate trust, authenticity, and connection with the public often find that perception can be a powerful tool in advancing their goals. Conversely, leaders who ignore or mishandle public opinion may be unable to effectively lead, regardless of their achievements or capabilities. Ultimately, successful leadership requires a deep understanding of how to manage policies and the perceptions and emotions of those being led.

Chapter 26: Mental Preparation

Preparation leads to success; this doesn't just refer to a plan for an event or job; it's also about mental preparation and toughness. These are crucial in helping leaders and individuals make better decisions under pressure. In high-stress environments, where decisions must be made quickly and accurately, mental toughness enables individuals to remain calm, focused, and resilient, ensuring they can think clearly and execute effective actions.

Mental toughness allows individuals to maintain focus and clarity during stressful situations. When emotions like fear, anxiety, or panic arise, mentally tough individuals can manage those emotions and stay grounded, allowing them to assess the situation logically and make informed decisions. Stress can cloud judgment and lead to rash or reactive decision-making. Mental preparation helps individuals build coping mechanisms that reduce the negative effects of stress. This enables them to remain composed and think through complex problems more efficiently. Mental toughness encourages adaptability in pressure-filled situations since conditions can change rapidly. Mentally prepared individuals are more likely to adjust their strategies based on new information rather than sticking rigidly to an initial plan, which improves decision quality. Mental toughness fosters self-confidence, which is critical in high-pressure scenarios. A mentally prepared individual believes in their ability to assess situations accurately and take decisive actions. This confidence enables them to make tough calls without hesitation, even under stressful conditions.

Setbacks and failures are inevitable under pressure. Mentally tough individuals are resilient, and they bounce back quickly. They learn from mistakes and continue making decisions without being paralyzed by previous errors. Visualize the outcome you want to achieve when there's a setback or too much pressure. Visualization is a powerful mental technique that involves mentally rehearsing scenarios and outcomes. By visualizing success or decision-making situations in advance, individuals prepare their minds to handle pressure more effectively. This process helps reduce anxiety, build confidence, and mentally rehearse complex decisions.

Positive visualization can help you regain perspective and motivate you to stay on course. Picture yourself successfully navigating a difficult situation. For example, if you're about to lead a critical meeting or face a difficult decision, visualize yourself remaining calm, analyzing the facts, and making a clear, effective choice. Imagine various potential scenarios you may face and practice responding to them in your mind. This mental exercise builds familiarity with high-pressure situations, making them less overwhelming when they occur in real life.

Once you have good visualization skills, you can mentally rehearse possible issues or questions you may face. This method involves repeatedly practicing decision-making and actions in your mind, much like an athlete would mentally rehearse a physical performance. By mentally simulating challenging situations, individuals can train their brains to respond composedly and strategically when the pressure hits.

Just like an athlete's warm-up with pregame rehearsal, before a significant decision or event, run through possible outcomes in your mind. For instance, mentally rehearse how you would respond to different arguments or offers if you are about to enter a negotiation. Remember to focus on managing your emotions during these mental rehearsals. Practice keeping calm, managing stress responses, and thinking even as the situation becomes more challenging.

Always plan for unknown variables; this helps develop a contingency plan. Contingency planning involves preparing for various potential outcomes and having backup plans. Knowing that you have thought through alternative courses of action in advance allows you to make quicker, more informed decisions under pressure, as you're not forced to come up with solutions on the spot. Analyze the potential risks and challenges you might face in a high-pressure scenario. Develop contingency plans for each risk so you're prepared to act when things are unplanned. Have at least two or three fallback options ready for any major decision. For example, if a project deadline is at risk, have alternative strategies for adjusting timelines, reallocating resources, or changing the scope of work to ensure you meet the goal. Circumstances can change, so it's important to regularly update your contingency plans based on new information or evolving risks.

Keeping your emotions under control is a large part of your success. Emotionally charged moments can lead to impulsive decisions. Mental toughness involves being aware of and controlling your emotions, particularly under stress. Emotional regulation lets you keep your emotions in check so they don't interfere with your logical decision-making process. Learn how to regulate your emotions by incorporating mindfulness techniques such as meditation, deep breathing, or progressive muscle relaxation, which can help reduce stress and keep your emotions stable. These practices promote calmness, which aids in making better decisions.

Before finalizing a decision in a high-pressure moment, take a few seconds to pause, breathe, and collect your thoughts. This brief reflection can help you reset your mind and prevent rash, emotion-driven decisions. This requires some stamina and mental toughness built through experience. Gradual exposure to stress in controlled environments helps individuals build resilience, allowing them to handle more significant challenges over time. The more you expose yourself to high-pressure situations, the more familiar and manageable they become.

Practice decision-making under controlled stress. For instance, you can create artificial deadlines, participate in mock scenarios, or set up high-stakes simulations that force you to make decisions quickly. Deliberately place yourself in uncomfortable or challenging situations to build resilience. Over time, what once felt overwhelming becomes manageable, and your ability to remain calm under pressure improves. In pressure-filled moments, it's easy to get overwhelmed by the magnitude of a situation or worry about the future. Mental toughness involves staying present and focusing on the immediate task rather than being distracted by the potential consequences.

Don't get overwhelmed in a situation; stay present in the moment and break the problems down into smaller ones. How do you eat an elephant? One bite at a time. Instead of focusing on the overall challenge, break the situation into smaller, manageable parts. Focus on solving one problem at a time, which prevents you from feeling overwhelmed. Focus on what you can control rather than stressing over things beyond your influence. This helps you maintain a sense of control and remain calm in high-stress situations.

Mental preparation and toughness are crucial for making sound decisions under pressure. Through visualization, mental rehearsals, and contingency planning, individuals can build the mental resilience needed to remain calm, focused, and adaptive in challenging situations. By preparing in advance and maintaining emotional control, leaders and professionals are better equipped to make thoughtful and strategic decisions, even when time is short and stakes are high. These techniques improve decision-making and contribute to long-term success by fostering mental resilience and confidence in the face of adversity.

Chapter 27: Manufactured Buy In

Leaders influence decision-making by framing choices; use strategic tactics for guiding a team to choose desired outcomes while empowering them. Guiding a team to choose desired outcomes while empowering them requires subtle yet effective leadership techniques focusing on influence rather than control. The key is to lead the team to believe the decision is theirs while subtly guiding them toward the best course of action. Many tactics and indirect leadership techniques can increase buy-in by presenting multiple viable options that have already been predetermined. Instead of presenting a single solution or direction, offer several options, each with merits. Ensure that the option you prefer is the most appealing. This way, the team feels free to choose, but the best choice is the one you want them to select. Suppose you want your team to adopt a new project management tool and present three different tools with comparative pros and cons. The one you prefer should have clear advantages like better functionality, ease of use, or more support for the team's specific needs.

Ask leading or strategic questions that lead your team to think critically and arrive at conclusions that align with your desired outcomes. Leading questions focus attention on the desired solution without imposing it outright. These questions can be as simple as "What do you think would happen if we focused more on quality than speed for this project?" or "How could adopting a more customer-centric approach improve our sales numbers?" These questions guide the conversation toward the desired outcomes while making the team feel like they decided independently, creating a sense of buy-in and ownership.

Another technique is framing the problem, not the solution. Clearly defining the problem or challenge allows the team to brainstorm solutions. However, the way you frame the problem can influence their thinking. If the problem has certain priorities, such as cost efficiency and innovation, the team will naturally lean toward solutions that align with those priorities. If you want the team to improve customer retention, frame the problem around customer satisfaction metrics and long-term value. The team will likely propose solutions focusing on areas that align with your desired outcome.

Explain the "why" to your team and highlight the benefits to the team. Your people are more likely to adopt ideas that they perceive will benefit them personally or as a group. When you position your preferred outcome in a way that highlights how it improves their work environment, personal growth, or team success, they are more likely to buy in. Knowing what motivates your people helps you develop this strategy. But, if you're proposing a change in workflow, explain how the new process will reduce their workload, enhance efficiency, or allow for more creativity in their roles. Show how the benefits directly affect their day-to-day experience.

Leaders also use data and evidence to support their preferred outcome. This is another subtle approach used by presenting data or case studies that support your desired goal. When people see evidence that a particular solution has worked elsewhere or has tangible benefits, they are more inclined to favor it. For example, if you want your team to adopt a new marketing strategy, present research and data from successful campaigns demonstrating the strategy's effectiveness. You make the solution more appealing without explicitly pushing it by showing results.

Encouraging ownership through delegation is a powerful way to empower your team while guiding them toward a specific outcome. Delegating certain responsibilities that lead them to the desired conclusion gives each member a sense of ownership in the outcome, increasing their drive and motivation to ensure the outcome is successful. When team members take ownership of parts of the decision-making process, they feel more invested in the outcome. Let's say you want to implement a new system, assign different team members to research various aspects of it, like its impact on workflow, costs, and training needs. When they present their findings, they may naturally advocate for the solution you prefer because they've discovered its value.

When building your team's buy-in, you can obtain subtle influences through strategically placing key team members on the team or in specific roles within the group. Sometimes, influencing key team members who have the trust and respect of the group can help guide the entire team toward the desired outcome. When these influencers support your idea, others are likely to follow suit. If one or two respected team members advocate for your preferred outcome, it creates a ripple effect. Work with these individuals beforehand, sharing your reasoning and data so they feel confident endorsing the solution to the rest of the team.

Another variable that you, as a leader, can control is time. This can be used to your benefit by creating a sense of urgency. Framing the situation as time-sensitive or showing the potential consequences of inaction, you can push the team toward quicker decision-making that aligns with your goals. Urgency often leads to a focus on practical, clear solutions, preferably the one you're proposing. For example, the statement, "If we don't implement this change now, we risk falling behind our competitors in the next quarter." or "Delaying this decision could increase costs by 20%." This tactic pressures the team to act swiftly and decisively, often leading them to adopt the most obvious or well-prepared solution (yours).

Involving the team in the development process is another way to increase buy-in; this helps the team shape the solution. People are more likely to support an idea they helped develop. Even if the general direction is predetermined, allowing the team to add their input makes them feel empowered. Let's say you're rolling out a new policy and invite the team to discuss the best implementation. They may tweak details, but they'll feel they have a say in how the change happens, even if the overall decision is already made.

Use positive reinforcement for any of the ideas the team develops. When team members offer ideas that align with your preferred outcome, reinforce those contributions with positive feedback. This signals to the group that these types of ideas are valued and can push the conversation toward the conclusion you desire. An example would be: "That's a great point, Sarah! That aligns perfectly with the direction we need to reach our goals."

Gene Kranz, flight director at NASA during the Apollo missions, often employed indirect leadership techniques, especially during the Apollo 13 crisis. Instead of dictating every solution, he allowed his engineers and flight controllers to suggest ideas and encouraged open brainstorming sessions. Kranz framed the problem clearly, "getting the astronauts home safely," and let his team take ownership of finding solutions. The team developed innovative solutions under immense pressure by fostering a culture of empowerment, trust, and collaboration. Though Kranz had a clear direction in mind, his indirect approach gave his team the autonomy to contribute, increasing their investment in successfully resolving the crisis.

The key to effectively guiding your team to choose the desired outcome while making them feel empowered is to influence their decision-making process without overtly controlling it. By offering options, asking the right questions, using evidence, and creating a sense of ownership, leaders can increase buy-in while allowing the team to feel autonomous. These indirect leadership techniques build trust and create a more collaborative environment where the team is aligned with your vision.

Chapter 28: Burn the Boats

There is an old saying, "If you want to take the island, burn the boats." This refers to leaving no option to return to where you came from. Total commitment breeds success, removing literal and metaphorical escape routes; this can push teams to perform at their highest level by creating an environment where there is no option for retreat or failure. This "burn the boats" mentality, where the only choice is to move forward, can foster creativity, resilience, and an intense focus on problem-solving. Leaders who embrace this all-or-nothing approach demonstrate that when teams are fully committed, they can achieve extraordinary results, often under pressure and in the face of adversity. When there is no option to turn back, teams must fully commit to the task. This laser focus on the objective helps eliminate distractions, complacency, and second-guessing. With no safety net, people become more resourceful and motivated to succeed, knowing failure is not an option. This strategy should only be used when the project or goal doesn't have flexibility in its schedule, and the team has been informed. This method is different from the previously discussed strategy of seeing opportunity in failure. Both strategies have their place and should be used strategically.

Teams are often more innovative in high-pressure situations where failure means significant loss. The absence of fallback plans forces individuals to think outside the box, explore unconventional solutions, and challenge existing assumptions. Without the comfort of retreat, people push their limits. Teams that work in an environment where the stakes are high and escape is not an option tend to develop stronger mental toughness. These teams learn to push through adversity, finding new reserves of endurance and determination. When excuses or easy ways out are unavailable, teams become more resilient, and success becomes a necessity rather than a possibility. In an all-or-nothing scenario, team members are more likely to pull together. Shared commitment to a singular goal and shared risk fosters a sense of unity. The pressure encourages people to rely on one another, often resulting in heightened collaboration, accountability, and trust.

The most famous example of removing escape routes, and where the saying derives from, Hernán Cortés, the Spanish conquistador. During his conquest of the Aztec Empire in 1519, Cortés famously ordered his men to burn their ships, leaving no option for retreat. By doing so, he forced his soldiers to confront the reality that their only way forward was to conquer. This bold and symbolic action instilled a sense of urgency and commitment in his men, leading to their eventual victory despite being vastly outnumbered. Though controversial in modern discussions, the "burn the boats" tactic is frequently cited as an example of how eliminating fallback options forces maximum effort and determination.

Elon Musk's leadership at Tesla and SpaceX reflects a modern example of removing escape routes. In 2008, both companies were on the verge of bankruptcy, and Musk invested nearly all his fortune in keeping them alive. There was no plan B; if Tesla failed, electric cars would lose a massive advocate, and if SpaceX failed, Musk's vision of reusable rockets and space exploration might be delayed for decades. Facing immense pressure, Musk and his teams were forced to innovate, creating the successful Falcon 1 rocket and launching the Tesla Model S. His willingness to risk everything pushed both teams to make history.

During World War II, Winston Churchill's leadership exemplified the all-or-nothing mentality. In 1940, after the fall of France, the U.K. was left isolated against Nazi Germany. Churchill famously refused to negotiate or consider surrender, even under the intense pressure of potential invasion. In his speech to Parliament, he declared, "We shall fight on the beaches, we shall fight on the landing grounds... we shall never surrender." Churchill galvanized the British people and military to stand firm by eliminating the possibility of giving in. His unwavering leadership was a critical factor in Britain's eventual victory, inspiring the country to endure despite overwhelming odds.

In 1914, explorer Ernest Shackleton and his crew were stranded in Antarctica after their ship, the Endurance, was crushed by ice. Shackleton faced an impossible situation with no clear escape.

Rather than allowing his men to despair, he forced them to focus on survival and relentless forward movement. Over nearly two years, Shackleton led his crew through harsh Antarctic conditions without losing a single man. Despite the bleak circumstances, his refusal to give up is a testament to the power of forcing teams to commit fully to a goal. Shackleton's leadership under extreme conditions remains a model of perseverance and resourcefulness.

While removing escape routes can unlock exceptional levels of performance, it can also backfire if not applied carefully. Leaders must assess when to use this approach, as it demands significant trust in the team's ability to cope under pressure. Poorly executed results in burnout, morale loss, and failure if the team is unprepared for the high stakes. With this strategy, leaders must understand that overreliance on an all-or-nothing mentality can overwhelm teams, leading to mistakes, burnout, or ethical lapses if people feel too much is at stake. Keeping escape routes open in some scenarios allows teams to pivot and adapt. Eliminating all fallback options can make leaders overly rigid when flexibility is crucial.

Leaders who embrace an all-or-nothing mentality can push their teams to extraordinary achievements by removing escape routes, fostering commitment, and forcing innovation. Bold leaders like Cortés, Musk, Churchill, and Shackleton understood that limiting options can unlock the highest potential in people by eliminating the fear of failure or retreat. However, the all-in approach must be balanced with consideration for the team's capacity and the potential risks involved. This strategy can transform how teams approach challenges and define their success under pressure.

Chapter 29: Window Vision

The metaphor of a window offers a powerful way to understand how vision creates clarity and transparency in leadership. Just as a window allows light to pass through, illuminating a space and offering a clear view of the outside world, a leader's vision provides a transparent framework through which team members can see the direction, goals, and values that guide their work. Vision, when communicated effectively, acts like a clear window free of distortions through which everyone can understand the purpose and destination of their collective efforts. The "window" also helps give perspective; if you're too close to the window, you can see a much broader picture on the other side, and conversely, if you're too far away from the window, you have a very narrow picture. Leaders need to determine how much of the picture they are looking at. Too much can overwhelm you sometimes, while too little leaves room for missing key aspects and could create failure.

A window allows for unobstructed views, just as a strong, well-articulated vision offers an unmistakable understanding of where the organization or team is headed. Clarity in vision enables team members to focus on shared goals, align their actions, and avoid confusion or distractions. Without a clear vision, people may lose their way, unable to see the bigger picture or understand how their efforts contribute to success. Apple's vision under Steve Jobs was clear: "to create the best user experience." This clarity of vision gave every department and employee a shared focus, helping to shape their decisions and innovations. The clarity of this vision empowered Apple to develop breakthrough products, as everyone had a clear understanding of what success looked like.

A window also signifies transparency; it allows people to see what lies beyond, creating trust. In leadership, transparency around vision ensures that team members are not confused about the future. When transparent about their vision, leaders foster a culture of openness and trust, where people feel more connected to the leader's intentions and the organization's purpose. Patagonia's vision to "save our home planet" is clear and transparent. The company communicates openly about its environmental goals and the challenges in the face of achieving them. This transparency builds trust among employees and customers, inspired by the company's commitment to its values and understands exactly what it stands for.

To offer the best view, a window must be clear and free from obstructions. Similarly, a vision should be simple and easy to understand. Leaders should avoid overly complex or jargon-heavy statements. A concise and straightforward vision is more likely to resonate with people, as they can quickly grasp its meaning and purpose. Boil down the vision into a single, memorable sentence or phrase that captures the essence of what you're aiming to achieve. Use clear language that is accessible to everyone in the organization. Google's vision is "to organize the world's information and make it universally accessible and useful." This simple, direct statement makes aligning with the company's broader goals easy for everyone, from engineers to marketers.

A window provides a view of the outside world but is also a part of the structure of a building. Similarly, a vision must be connected to the day-to-day actions of the team. Leaders should regularly communicate how individual tasks and team efforts contribute to the larger vision. This linkage helps employees see the relevance of their work and fosters a deeper commitment to achieving the overall goals. Regularly explain how specific projects or tasks fit into the bigger picture. Make the connection between daily work and the long-term vision explicit so team members understand the value of their contributions. At Tesla, Elon Musk continually reinforces how each innovation and technological breakthrough contributes to the company's vision of accelerating the world's transition to sustainable energy. This consistent communication helps employees see how their work impacts the broader mission.

Just as windows can be opened to allow fresh air in, a vision must allow space for team input. Involving the team in shaping or refining the vision can create a sense of ownership and commitment. When people feel that they've contributed to the creation of the vision, they are more likely to be invested in its success. Engage the team in discussions about the vision during its development. Solicit feedback and ideas from employees and ensure they feel their input matters. This participatory approach helps ensure the vision resonates with the entire organization. Southwest Airlines involves employees in shaping its culture and operational vision. This inclusion has resulted in a highly committed workforce connected to the company's goals, leading to better performance and customer service.

A window must be regularly cleaned to maintain clarity. Similarly, a vision must be consistently communicated and reinforced to stay at the forefront of everyone's mind. Leaders should integrate the vision into all aspects of communication, such as meetings, emails, and performance reviews. Frequent reminders help keep the vision alive and relevant. Embed the vision in everyday communication. Refer to it in meetings, newsletters, and public addresses. Celebrate successes that align with the vision and use setbacks as opportunities to reinforce the importance of staying true to the long-term goal. Howard Schultz frequently spoke about Starbucks' mission to inspire and nurture the human spirit, from employee interactions to customer service. This continual reinforcement helped Starbucks employees understand and embody the company's vision daily.

The view through the window should match what's on the other side; leaders must align their actions with their vision. When leaders consistently align with their vision, they build credibility and inspire others to do the same. Authenticity is key to maintaining clarity and trust. Model the behavior and decisions that reflect the vision.

Leaders should demonstrate commitment to the vision in their actions and decisions, showing that it's not just words but a driving force behind everything they do. Satya Nadella exemplifies Microsoft's vision of empowering individuals and organizations through technology. His leadership style, which emphasizes empathy, learning, and collaboration, directly aligns with this vision, making him a credible and inspiring figure to employees and stakeholders.

A window shows the outside world, including any obstacles or challenges. Leaders should be similarly transparent about the organization's challenges in pursuing its vision. This honesty builds trust and allows teams to prepare for difficulties while remaining focused on the goal. Communicate openly about potential setbacks, roadblocks, or uncertainties in achieving the vision. Acknowledge the difficulties but frame them as opportunities for learning and growth, showing confidence in the team's ability to overcome them. When Shopify's CEO Tobias Lütke faced difficult business decisions during the COVID-19 pandemic, he communicated transparently with employees about the challenges and uncertainties while reaffirming the company's long-term vision. His honesty helped maintain employee morale and trust.

The window metaphor highlights the importance of clarity and transparency in leadership. A vision must be communicated simply and directly connected to everyday work. By maintaining transparency, involving the team, and consistently reinforcing the vision, leaders can ensure that everyone understands and is aligned with the organization's goals; just like a window that offers an unobstructed view, a well-communicated vision allows teams to see the path ahead clearly while trusting in the leadership that guides them.

Chapter 30: Failure is Good

Failure is an excellent learning tool; embrace it! Failure can be one of the most powerful catalysts for growth and improvement. While it may initially seem like a setback, failure provides opportunities for learning, innovation, and resilience. By embracing failure as a natural and essential part of the growth process, individuals and organizations can use it as a stepping stone to success. Failure offers a unique opportunity to reflect on what went wrong, why it happened, and what can be done differently. Mistakes provide valuable feedback, helping to identify gaps in strategy, skills, or execution. By analyzing failures, individuals and teams can develop better solutions, improve processes, and prevent similar issues in the future. Thomas Edison famously failed thousands of times before inventing the lightbulb. He viewed each failure as a step toward discovering what didn't work, which ultimately led to his success. His perseverance and willingness to learn from failure allowed him to innovate continuously.

Experiencing failure teaches individuals how to handle adversity and bounce back from setbacks. Over time, facing and overcoming failure builds emotional resilience, making people more capable of handling future challenges with composure and determination. Oprah Winfrey was fired early in her career as a television reporter for being "unfit for TV." Instead of being discouraged, she used the experience to fuel her drive and eventually became one of history's most successful media personalities. Her resilience in the face of early setbacks allowed her to grow and thrive.

Don't create a culture that fears failure; encourage it! Failure often sparks innovation. When traditional methods fail, it forces individuals and teams to think creatively and explore new approaches. Many groundbreaking innovations arise from trial and error; initial failures lead to unexpected solutions or opportunities. The development of Post-it notes by 3M resulted from a failed experiment to create a super-strong adhesive. Instead of discarding the failed project, 3M saw the potential in the weak adhesive, eventually turning it into one of their most successful products.

Failure also teaches humility and self-awareness by revealing limitations or areas for improvement. It forces individuals to confront their shortcomings, and through this process, they can become more reflective, open to feedback, and focused on personal growth. J.K. Rowling, the author of the "Harry Potter" series, faced multiple rejections from publishers before her work was finally accepted. She has spoken openly about how her early failures shaped her, teaching her humility, perseverance, and self-belief, which ultimately contributed to her success.

Failure requires individuals to go back to the drawing board and think critically about how to solve problems more effectively. This improves their analytical skills and ability to approach challenges from different angles, resulting in stronger, more well-rounded problem-solving abilities. The Wright brothers faced numerous failures and crashes before successfully achieving powered flight. Each setback forced them to go back and improve their designs, ultimately leading to their historic breakthrough in aviation.

Learn how to embrace failure as part of the process and redefine failure as an essential part of the learning and growth process rather than a reflection of personal or professional inadequacy. View failure as a temporary condition, not an outcome. Remember that failure is a stepping stone to success and a sign that you are challenging yourself. Instead of asking, "Why did I fail?" ask, "What can I learn from this experience?" This shift in thinking can help you view failure more positively and as an opportunity for growth.

Leaders can foster a culture that encourages experimentation and risk-taking by creating an environment where failure is not stigmatized but embraced as part of the innovation process. Employees should feel safe to take calculated risks and share their failures openly, knowing that the focus will be on learning, not blame. As a leader, celebrate failures as learning experiences. Encourage employees to share stories of what went wrong and what they learned and highlight how these lessons will form future success. After a failure, take the time to analyze what went wrong, why it happened, and what can be improved. Use the experience as a postmortem to gather insights and identify growth areas. This reflection process helps ensure that failure leads to improvement rather than repeated mistakes. Afterward, develop a structured process for analyzing failures. Ask key questions such as, "What assumptions were wrong?" "What can we do differently next time?" or "What have we learned about our process, market, or team?"

Failure can be discouraging, but persistence is essential for long-term success. Many of the world's most successful individuals faced significant failures early in their careers but refused to give up. Resilience is about pushing through setbacks and staying focused on your ultimate goals. After experiencing failure, keep your long-term vision in mind when facing failure. Remember that setbacks are temporary, and each failure brings you closer to success. Break large challenges into smaller, manageable tasks to maintain momentum after failure. While failure can lead to growth, taking calculated risks worth the potential downside is important. Evaluate the risks before acting and be prepared to pivot if things don't go as planned. This approach allows you to fail without causing significant damage and encourages experimentation within safe boundaries. Adopt an 80/20 rule for risk-taking, where 80% of your efforts are focused on proven strategies and 20% are dedicated to innovative, experimental approaches. This way, your efforts remain on track even if the experiment fails.

Foster a growth mindset, personally and within your team, emphasizing that abilities and intelligence can be developed through hard work, learning, and perseverance. This mindset encourages people to embrace challenges, learn from feedback, and see failure as an opportunity to improve rather than a threat. Focus on effort and progress rather than innate talent or success. Encourage yourself and others to view setbacks as challenges to overcome rather than reflections of fixed abilities.

It's important to be kind to yourself when facing failure. Self-compassion involves acknowledging that failure is a part of the human experience and treating yourself with understanding and patience. This helps prevent feelings of self-blame or discouragement from stifling future efforts. When failure occurs, remind yourself that even the most successful people fail. Take a break, reflect, and reengage with renewed energy and a clear mind. It helps to document and track your failures and what you learned from them. Documenting failures helps you see how much you've grown and reminds you that progress often comes from learning what doesn't work. This record can serve as a valuable reference point for future decision-making. Keep a failure journal to document your failures, what went wrong, and the key takeaways. Reviewing this journal periodically can offer insights into patterns and help you make better decisions in the future.

While often uncomfortable, failure is an essential part of growth and improvement. By shifting our mindset, learning from mistakes, and staying resilient, failure becomes a valuable tool for success. Great leaders and innovators, from Thomas Edison to J.K. Rowling, have demonstrated that embracing failure as part of the process leads to greater achievement, innovation, and personal growth.

180

Ultimately, failure is not something to be feared but embraced as a necessary part of the journey toward excellence.

Chapter 31: Self Failures

Failures can be used to build trust through transparency. Admitting failures as a leader is a crucial part of effective leadership. It demonstrates accountability, honesty, and a willingness to learn from mistakes. Rather than diminishing a leader's authority, owning up to failures can build trust with team members and stakeholders, turning those moments into valuable teaching opportunities. Leaders who openly discuss their failures foster a culture of transparency, encourage risk taking and innovation while setting an example of resilience.

Timing is critical when admitting failure; the longer a leader waits to acknowledge a mistake, the more likely it is that others will discover it first, potentially damaging trust. Admitting failure promptly shows responsibility and transparency, allowing the team to start focusing on solutions rather than assigning blame. CEO Akio Toyoda addressed the issue head-on after Toyota's 2010 massive recall due to faulty parts. He admitted the company's failure to ensure safety, publicly apologized, and promised to take corrective actions to regain trust. Toyoda helped restore faith in Toyota's brand by acting quickly and accepting responsibility.

Generalized admissions of failure do not hold the same weight as being clear and specific. A good leader will outline what went wrong, what decisions or assumptions led to the failure, and the consequences. Being open about the specific factors behind the mistake shows depth of understanding and willingness to learn. After the failure of Google Glass, Sundar Pichai, then a senior leader at Google and now CEO of Alphabet, acknowledged that the product's rollout was rushed and not fully thought through, especially regarding market readiness and public perception. Pichai emphasized that the failure provided valuable insights for the company's future approach to augmented reality and wearable technology.

Own it!!! A key part of leadership is owning the responsibility for the team's failures, even if the leader wasn't directly involved. Shifting blame to team members or external factors erodes trust and morale. By owning the failure, leaders can demonstrate integrity and accountability, fostering a culture where team members feel safe to take risks without fear of blame. President Obama took full responsibility after the disastrous launch of the healthcare.gov website, stating, "There's no excuse for the problems, and they are my responsibility." He followed up by directing resources to fix the issue, eventually turning the platform around. Obama's willingness to own the failure as the administration's leader helped restore public trust.

As many great leaders learn from other's mistakes, leaders can turn failures into teaching moments by framing them as learning experiences. Acknowledging what went wrong and explaining what can be learned encourages a growth mindset within the team. This not only helps in avoiding the same mistakes but also promotes continuous improvement. In 2009, Netflix's CEO Reed Hastings announced the launch of "Qwikster," a separate DVD rental service that was intended to split from Netflix's streaming service. The move was met with massive customer backlash, and Hastings quickly admitted that it was a mistake, saying they "lacked insight" into what their customers wanted. He used the failure as an opportunity to rethink Netflix's strategy and customer service approach, ultimately leading to its massive success in streaming. This transparency earned Hasting's respect, as he demonstrated his ability to learn from mistakes.

Admitting failure isn't enough on its own; leaders must also outline a clear path forward, explaining the steps to prevent similar failures in the future. Offering a solution reassures the team that the problem is being addressed and turns the failure into a constructive part of the company's growth. After Starbucks' 2008 downturn, Howard Schultz admitted that the company had over-expanded and lost its focus on the customer experience. He did not just apologize; he closed underperforming stores, revamped operations, and launched new initiatives focused on reconnecting with customers. Schultz's handling of this failure revitalized Starbucks, and his recovery plan was crucial to its long-term success.

After admitting a failure, leaders should encourage their teams to reflect on the situation and offer input. This promotes a collaborative culture and helps ensure that everyone learns from failure, fostering a sense of ownership and accountability throughout the organization. When NASA faced the Challenger disaster in 1986, leadership didn't shy away from the failure. Following the tragedy, they encouraged team reflection through the Rogers Commission investigation, which identified key decision-making errors. This transparency and openness to input transformed NASA's safety protocols and ultimately strengthened the organization, restoring public trust in the agency.

Jack Ma, the founder of Alibaba, faced numerous failures in creating one of the world's largest e-commerce platforms. He famously applied to dozens of jobs and was repeatedly rejected. Alibaba faced several early setbacks, including a failed expansion into the U.S. market. Ma consistently admitted these failures, framing them as learning experiences that fueled Alibaba's future success. His transparency about failure made him relatable and helped him build trust with investors and employees.

Spanx founder Sara Blakely credits her success to her ability to embrace failure. She often shares how her father encouraged her to talk about her failures at the dinner table when she was young, which helped her develop a mindset that saw mistakes as valuable learning experiences. Blakely has turned this mentality into a cornerstone of Spanx's company culture, promoting innovation and risk-taking. Her openness about failure has earned her a reputation as an authentic and relatable leader.

J.K. Rowling, author of the Harry Potter series, has openly discussed her struggles with failure. Before achieving global success, Rowling faced multiple rejections from publishers and dealt with personal hardships. Her openness about these setbacks, especially in her famous 2008 Harvard commencement speech, resonated with millions. She framed her failures as necessary steps to discovering her true potential. Rowling's willingness to be vulnerable about her failures has built a deep connection and trust with her audience.

Before becoming the 16th president of the United States, Abraham Lincoln experienced numerous political failures, including several elections losses. He never hid from these failures, often discussing them publicly and using them to refine his approach to leadership. Lincoln's resilience and ability to learn from failure eventually led him to the presidency, where he demonstrated the same qualities in navigating the country through the Civil War. His openness about failure, built trust and credibility, making him one of America's most revered leaders.

Admitting failures as a leader is not a sign of weakness but rather an opportunity to build trust, foster growth, and inspire others. Leaders who openly acknowledge mistakes show their teams that failure is a natural part of the process and can lead to growth if handled properly. By admitting failures promptly, taking responsibility, framing them as learning experiences, and providing

186

a clear plan for moving forward, leaders can turn setbacks into powerful teaching moments. Leaders like Hastings, Schultz, Rowling, Lincoln and Blakely have all demonstrated how owning failure can strengthen relationships with employees and stakeholders while driving long-term success.

Chapter 32: Resourcefulness

Successful leaders are experts at identifying and maximizing internal and external resources essential for efficient functioning and growth. Whether it's talent within the team, technology, finances, or external partnerships, knowing how to leverage these resources effectively can improve performance, productivity, and innovation. Internal resources are assets that exist within the organization, such as human capital, which could be skillsets or expertise. Every team member brings unique talents, skills, and experiences. Identifying strengths in leadership, creativity, technical skills, or problem-solving can help assign roles that maximize each person's potential. Identifying these requires regular assessments, skills inventories, performance reviews, and open communication with employees can help uncover hidden talents and expertise.

Along with human capital, assessing the existing software, hardware, and technological infrastructure can reveal tools that may be underutilized. Conduct audits of current systems and tools and gather employee feedback on their effectiveness. Internal processes, such as workflow systems, supply chain management, and operational protocols, are critical resources that can be optimized for efficiency. Review operational efficiency through metrics like production time, costs, or bottlenecks, and encourage input from team members who are directly involved.

External resources are those outside the organization, such as industry partnerships and collaborations. Partnering with other organizations for joint ventures, research, or supply chain management can increase capacity and expertise. Identifying these by attending industry events, conferences or joining associations to identify potential partners is key to using these resources. Keep an eye on competitors and complementary businesses that could offer collaboration opportunities. Consultants and freelancers are also external assets to be leveraged. Hiring external experts to fill skill gaps or provide temporary support can be a cost-effective way to gain specialized knowledge without a long-term commitment. To find experts, external resource platforms can be used such as LinkedIn, Upwork, or industry-specific consultant networks.

There are not many organizations out there that do not require financial resources. Grants, investors, and financial institutions can provide additional capital for growth or innovation. Research government grants, private equity funds, and venture capital networks. Building relationships with financial institutions and investors helps increase external resources.

An underutilized resource is educational institutions, partnering with universities or training programs for research, talent acquisition, or innovation projects can be an extremely valuable

189

resource. Contact academic institutions for internships, collaborative projects, or access to emerging technologies and talent pools. This is the same with external partnerships; by leveraging these partnerships, you can collaborate to gain access to expertise or technology that you don't have in-house. Strategic partnerships can reduce costs, speed production, and open new markets.

Effective leaders understand the importance of talent management. Your goal should match team members' strengths to appropriate roles and projects. Provide training and development opportunities to further enhance their skills, which ensures that people are working at their highest capacity and continuously growing. People and tools are only successful if they are being used most effectively. Ensure that internal tools are being fully utilized. Invest in technology upgrades when necessary to enhance productivity. Cloud-based software, AI tools, and automation can drastically increase efficiency. Regularly evaluate operational systems and workflows to identify inefficiencies. Look for opportunities to automate repetitive tasks or streamline processes to save time and resources.

Networking is critical for both identifying and maximizing external resources. It allows leaders and organizations to build relationships that open doors to new opportunities, whether finding new talent, exploring partnerships, or gaining insights from industry peers. Networking allows you a connection to the knowledge and experience of others. Whether learning from the successes and failures of other leaders or gaining access to new strategies, networking provides access to a wealth of information. Through networking, you can find potential partners for collaborations or joint ventures that can expand your capabilities or reach new markets. A strong professional network can be a great source for discovering new talent or securing expert advice on hiring practices. Networking can help keep you informed about industry trends, modern technologies, and shifts in market demands, enabling you to make informed decisions for the organization's growth.

Delegating is essential for maximizing internal resources and improving team productivity. It empowers employees, prevents burnout, and ensures leaders can focus on strategic initiatives rather than getting bogged down in day-to-day tasks. Delegation increases efficiency; it allows leaders to focus on high-priority work while trusting team members to manage other tasks. This optimizes time and resources, ensuring people work on the right tasks. Delegating responsibilities allows employees to take on new challenges, develop skills, and gain experience. It fosters a sense of ownership and accountability, helping employees grow in their roles. Leaders can make better strategic decisions when they delegate operational tasks. Delegating allows more focus on long-term planning, growth strategies, and innovation. When leaders delegate, it shows trust in the team's abilities; this builds employee confidence and encourages them to take initiative, be creative, and feel more invested in the organization's success. One very important part about delegation to remember is that you may delegate certain responsibilities or jobs, but you, as the leader, are still responsible for the overall outcome.

Identifying and maximizing internal and external resources is vital to an organization's success. Effective resource management ensures that talent, technology, and partnerships are leveraged for maximum impact. Networking provides opportunities for growth and collaboration while delegating empowers teams, fostering a culture of ownership and high performance. Combining these approaches allows leaders to optimize resources, enhance productivity, and drive sustainable success.

Chapter 33: Embrace the Suck

Leaders are rarely judged on the good times but on their performance during tough times. Embracing hardship is critical in developing stronger leaders because it fosters resiliency, adaptability, and mental toughness. Leaders who can navigate challenges and adversity emerge with valuable experience and strength that enhances their ability to guide others, make tough decisions, and remain focused under pressure. Leaders who face and overcome adversity become more resilient. Hardship teaches them how to recover from setbacks and manage stress effectively, which is crucial in navigating the uncertainties of leadership. Difficult experiences force leaders to think creatively and adapt their strategies. They develop the ability to make quick, sound decisions under pressure, which is critical in demanding environments. Fostering an environment of empathy and emotional intelligence can help leaders who endure hardship, gain a deeper understanding of struggle, enabling them to better relate to their teams. This empathy enhances emotional intelligence, a key trait for effective leadership in managing diverse teams and challenges. By facing difficulties, leaders build confidence in their abilities. Knowing they can manage tough situations empowers them to take calculated risks and trust their instincts, which are essential for strong decision-making. Hardship often forces leaders to confront their values and ethics. Those who emerge from adversity with integrity tend to gain trust and respect from their teams, fostering a culture of accountability and building mental toughness. Individuals must cultivate mental toughness to thrive in adversity and become stronger leaders.

Embracing a growth mindset means viewing challenges as learning opportunities rather than threats. Leaders who believe they can grow through hardship are likelier to persist through difficulties and emerge stronger. Mental toughness comes from consistent practice in self-discipline. Leaders can build this by setting goals, maintaining focus, and sticking to their plans even when motivation wanes. Regular exercise, mindfulness, and disciplined work routines contribute to mental fortitude. Leaders must train themselves to step outside their comfort zones. This could involve taking on new challenges, learning new skills, or tackling difficult conversations. Repeatedly pushing boundaries builds endurance and mental strength. Effective leaders learn to manage stress through mindfulness, meditation, breathing exercises, or journaling. These techniques help them stay calm, focused, and emotionally balanced during crises. Leaders with mental toughness don't get easily discouraged by short-term setbacks. Instead, they stay focused on long-term goals. Leaders can maintain motivation and direction during challenging times by developing the ability to see past immediate obstacles and work toward a larger purpose. Mentally tough leaders view failure not as a defeat but as a learning experience. They use failures to refine their strategies, gain insight, and grow in wisdom. This mindset helps them move forward instead of dwelling on setbacks. While mental toughness involves self-reliance, seeking support from mentors, peers, and team members is equally important. Strong leaders are not afraid to seek help or guidance when needed and actively seek feedback to improve. Reflecting on past hardships and how they overcame them reinforces a leader's mental resilience. It allows them to draw strength from past experiences and apply those lessons to future challenges. One example of mental toughness and resilience would be President Donald Trump. His journey in politics has been marked by a determined resilience, facing numerous challenges head-on. Through shifting public opinion, legal battles, and intense scrutiny, he has shown an unyielding drive, often leveraging these challenges to solidify his stance and motivate his base. Despite facing formidable opposition, Trump has maintained a commitment to his ideals and goals, illustrating his ability to persist in the face of adversity. His resilience has often been a defining aspect of his public image, showcasing his capacity to adapt, rebound, and remain a prominent figure in American politics.

Hardship, while difficult, is one of the most effective ways to forge strong leaders. It forces individuals to grow beyond their limits, develop critical skills, and build the mental toughness necessary to lead others through adversity. By embracing challenges, cultivating resilience, and developing difficult hardship strategies for mental toughness, leaders can enhance their ability to navigate difficult circumstances and drive long-term success.

As we reach the closing pages of this journey through the essence of effective leadership, let us reflect on what we've uncovered. Leadership is not an exclusive trait reserved for the few; it is an evolving skill, a commitment, and a mindset accessible to anyone willing to embrace it. Effective leadership begins with the belief that every person has the potential to lead, whether on a small team, in a family, or on the grandest stages of business, military, or community life.

We've explored how effective leadership isn't about having all the answers or unlimited resources. Rather, it's about using the tools, knowledge, and resources available to achieve the best possible outcome. A true leader recognizes the power in what they already possess, from the strengths of their team members to the tools and technologies within their reach. They don't wait for ideal conditions but thrive within the constraints of reality, adapting and finding creative solutions along the way.

Most importantly, the will to lead effectively is essential. It's not about simply taking charge, but about shouldering responsibility, serving others, and staying committed through challenging times. Leadership demands resilience, the courage to make difficult decisions, and the humility to seek help and recognize growth areas.

Ultimately, remember that anyone can step into the role of a leader. It requires effort, yes, but it also calls for authenticity, empathy, and a relentless desire to uplift others. The journey is ongoing, filled with lessons to learn and moments to inspire. Embrace the tools you have, trust in your potential, and lead with a heart committed to growth for yourself and those you guide. The world needs more leaders, and the opportunity is always there for those who are willing. The choice to lead, to make a difference, and to inspire change rests with each of us.

Acknowledgments

First and foremost, I want to thank my family, both blood and Navy. I have been blessed with the life that I don't feel I deserve, and I am truly humbled and thankful. The United States Navy gave me a career and opportunity that I could never have dreamed of and has exposed me to so many incredible people.

The idea of this book stems from feedback I have received from many of the people I've encountered throughout my career that told me I should write a book. My answer to it was always one of those passing jokes "maybe someday". During my last tour I was privileged enough to have a mix of Sailors and Civilians that I worked beside and gave me the encouragement to give back by sharing lessons I've learned. My heartfelt thanks go to all the leaders who have taken time to invest in me. Your guidance and wisdom are engraved throughout these pages, and I thank you all.

I can't accurately express in words the absolute pleasure it's been working with so many incredible Navy Chiefs, who have helped instill the honor, courage and commitment to write this book. They deserve the credit for this book.

Thank you to everyone who bought this book and I hope that it benefits you in your goal of becoming an effective leader.

About the Author

Frank M. Kuras was born and raised in Coventry, Rhode Island, where he developed a strong sense of commitment and service from an early age. In 2003, he answered the call to serve by enlisting in the United States Navy, beginning a career marked by dedication, resilience, and an unwavering sense of duty. Over the years, Frank's journey has taken him across the globe, where he has honed his skills, embraced leadership, and embodied the core values of the Navy.

Throughout his distinguished career, Frank has served in a variety of challenging and diverse roles. His early assignments included time on the USS Ashland (LSD-48), where he gained invaluable experience working aboard an amphibious dock landing ship. Following this, he served with the Navy's elite fighting force, the Navy SEALs at Logistic Support Unit 2 (LOGSU), further developing his expertise in critical planning and operations. Later, he joined SEAL Delivery Vehicle (SDV) Team 1, a unique role that required the highest level of operational readiness and collaboration with elite units. His assignments have also included a tour at the Naval Undersea Warfare Center (NUWC), where he contributed to advancements in undersea systems, as well as aboard the USS Fitzgerald (DDG-62), a guided-missile destroyer, where he served with distinction. His current role at the Naval Surface Warfare Center in Picatinny reflects his continued commitment to innovation and support of the Navy's mission.

Frank's commitment to leadership excellence is also reflected in his academic achievements. He holds a Master's degree in strategic leadership from the University of Charleston, West Virginia, equipping him with advanced insights into leadership and organizational dynamics. Additionally, he is a graduate of the Navy's Senior Enlisted Academy, a rigorous program that prepares senior enlisted leadership for the highest levels of responsibility and influence within the Navy.

With over two decades of service, Frank M. Kuras's career embodies the dedication, integrity, and resilience that define a lifelong commitment to the Navy. As a Senior Chief Petty Officer, he continues to inspire and lead, always upholding the Navy's highest standards and setting an example for future generations of Warfighters.

www.ingramcontent.com/pod-product-compliance
Lightning Source LLC
Chambersburg PA
CBHW061153120626
46546CB00005B/2040